Paddle to Paddle

Lois Chapin

Nightingale Rose Publications

Yorba Linda 2019

Acknowledgements

I wish to thank all those who were instrumental in making this book of poetry happen, including The Los Angeles Poets & Writers Collective and Jack Grapes, as well as Chiwan Choi, Baz Here, Bambi Here, Dave Barton, Laura Border, my Imua ohana, my sweetheart, Mike, and our four kids.

Disclaimer:

NR Nightingale Rose Publications

16960 E. Bastanchury Rd.

Yorba Linda, CA 92886

© 2019 Nightingale Rose Publications

All rights reserved

ISBN 13: 978-1-889755-10-6

ISBN 10: 1-88975-01-9

Library of Congress Catalogue: TX 8-696-1521

If you want to change the world, find someone to help you paddle.
–William H. McRaven

Dedicated to those who found a way out.

Contents

Paddle to Paddle

Proverbs 29:15

Seems like Jesus' mom
was cool.
Encouraged him to argue,
and disagree,
let him hang out
with older friends,
and disappear for days
at a time,
allowed him to live at home
through his twenties
and make mind-altering substances.
She even believed
everything he said,
and didn't believe
an unpaddled child
disgraces his mother.
If only Mary
had written
Child Guidance,
and not Ellen,
the cult leader.

Home

"You're so heavy!"
It's the first time I've ever seen you.
I'm trying not to move in my wooden rocking chair
with the cut-out heart
and two red bird stencils.
I guess they're supposed to be nightingales.
That's your name now too.
Daddy put you in my arms.
You're lying on my lap,
your head on my arm.
He told me to be careful
not to drop you.
You're a lot bigger than I thought.
Your blanket is so soft.
Oops,
that's your pacifier on the floor
by my foot.
Mommy left for a long time
to get you out of her stomach.
She was sick.
She almost died.
She had *toxemia*.
It's from not eating good
when growing a baby.
Sorry you got sick too.
Daddy said you were born blue
with a rope or something wrapped
around your neck,
twice.
You had to stay in the hospital
after Mommy came home
to make you well. I'm glad
you're okay. I hope
you don't have to go back
too much more. Maybe Mommy
will be nicer since
you're here.
In the mornings before Daddy
goes to work at the lab he eats

boiled potatoes with salt.
I ask for a bite,
but he says I need a better breakfast
and makes me eat Ruskets.
I hope he doesn't get sick
from eating cold potatoes.
Great Grandma Mimi played
with me
while I've been waiting
for you. She takes me
for walks in my stroller with Baby Doll
by the canal.
Baby Doll is a lot lighter than you.
Her eyes open
and close
and are blue
like yours.
I've never seen real blue eyes before.
"Your eyes are so blue!"
When you talk,
I'll teach you stuff.
Mommy'll want you
to call her "Mummy."
That's what Moses' pharaoh was called,
so I call
her "Mamma."
When you're bigger you can go outside
with me
when she gets mad and makes me
leave the house.
We'll catch snails. I'm good
at catching them
in the front yard so Mommy
can rest.
I'll show you how
to put them in empty peanut butter jars.
Boys are supposed
to like that stuff.
Your hands are so tiny. You grip my finger
so strong!
There's no one to play with

when Daddy's at work.
I can't wait 'til you're bigger
and can play.
Click! Poof!
That's Daddy,
he takes
pictures of everything.
Those flash bulbs
won't hurt you, you just see white dots
for a while.
He goes to school at night and works
at the hospital in the daytime.
He drives
the car.
We live up on a big hill.
Mommy doesn't
drive so we stay up here
and take naps. Looks like you like sleeping,
so,
that's good.
Sometimes they fight
real loud.
I don't know
about what.
But when they ask you which one
is right, it's best
not to answer.
She'll get mad at you
no matter which side
you take.

She has some stickers
of little children
of the world,
she sings
a song about them too.
Anyway,
you lick the back and stick them
on paper.
But don't touch them unless
she gives them to you.

She hits just like she's cleaning
a carpet.

"Can I show him the pollywogs
in the canal?"
I guess everything is
after you get bigger.
"Can I feed him
so he gets bigger
faster?"

Safe

Only one relative from either side
ever left us anything
in a will.
A conman and a drug dealer,
well, he ran bootleg
as a kid after his family lived in a box car,
he graduated up to selling the hard stuff.
Anyway, when colon cancer killed
my grandfather at the VA
he left my mom enough
ill-earned green
to add on to the most important
room of the house,
the study.
Books from carpet to ceiling
and two desks pressed into our den.
A secret portal waited
under my father's desk.
I pulled the chair back in
after I hid there.
The wood smell tickled my nose;
I had to be careful not to bump
my head
on the drawer glides.
But the best was
the safe.
The smaller safe of course, the one
we were supposed to show robbers
my mother said
if we were held at gun point
in a home invasion.
The closet hid the big safe.
Heaven was where
we were supposed to store up treasure,
I guess ours waited in the big safe
for Brinks to get
it up there.
I spun the notched knob of the safe
with my fingers.

Clunk, clunk the tumblers clunk
unseen
as I turned the cylinder over
the white painted lines
between 5 and 10
and back over 30 and 40.
A bandana robber
from the wild west took
control of my hand.
My horse, tethered outside the bank, stomped
waiting for saddle bags
filled with gold nuggets.
Great gold nuggets
like sheep brains
with knotty cortexes
gold nuggets that gleamed in the sun. Prospectors believed
this bank was safe, Ha!
A car backfires
on the freeway. The sheriff shoots
my lookout in the front of the bank
blocking my escape. I need to drag
these overfilled saddlebags.
The wood plank floor boards smell
of varnish.
An Indian penny winks
up at me through the dust.
My heart beats tom toms
in my ears.
The 91 freeway always has traffic.
I hear Slippered Feet, the deputy
shuffle
down the hall, it's now
or never.
I dart for cover under
my mother's desk. The sound of papers
crumpling
threatens to give me away.
Pogo, Bugs Bunny, Tom and Jerry
comic books sprawl
over buck-tooth *Mad* magazine covers, and shiny
Playgirl Centerfolds

tumble from the piles stacked
to the pine drawer gliders.
There's no room to squeeze
against the pillars of newsprint
with my saddle bags.
The silver tip of a fountain pen impales
the shag carpet.
I'll never make it to my loyal appaloosa.
She's pawing the ground. Her whinnies urge
me on. She'll gallop
me away from this corrupt
sheriff town out to the freedom
of the desert.
It's not a mirage.
These gold nuggets will buy me
all I need.
Cacti hold survival water.
"Move over," my brother says.
"This is my spot!"
I give him
a shoulder shove.
It's too tight for both of us
and wrinkled magazines tear in our scuffle.
Maybe
he's after my gold
or wants to escape
on my horse.
Another gun shot.
I'm hit.
"Take the bags," I say
and I clutch my chest.
Blood spurts.
I look to see
if it is separated. Separated blood means
you're dead.
"What bags?" he asks.
"The ones with the gold nuggets,
like sheep brains."
I leave him to read the forbidden cache of comics
and crawl wounded
back under my father's desk.

The knob clicks
as I turn it.
The door still won't open. I spin
it faster, it's my only chance
for escape.
Safety, and my outlaw grandfather
who I don't know,
lie on the other side.
I just need to guess
the right
combination.

Fishhook

I poke the fishhook through the pink fish egg.
Pop.
It's like giant caviar.
Not that I'd eat caviar.
My brother and I are being raised
vegetarians. like Daddy.
She's a carnivore.
We are fishing for her.
The planks of the pier are rough
under my bare feet.
The water ripples a clear blue.
I pull up my rod
and thump the red and white float
with my finger.
It's tied above the round grey weight.
Another vacation.
We left the house at two in the morning,
rolled onto the freeway after hours
of her smacking us and threatening
we wouldn't go at all, while we packed
the camper and thirteen-foot trailer.
This,
of course,
as all vacations,
was going to be
our
very
last
one.

I hang my pink fish egg over the water.
Daddy's shown me how to press
the button on my rod and release it after
I cast out.
"Poor Mummy" is resting in the trailer
drawing cartoons.
I push the button and swing
the rod
and all its decorations

18

over my shoulder.
I like how it bends
when I swing it. I fling it back
over the water and lift my finger
from the button.

Screams.

I'm confused.
The line doesn't hit
the water.
There's tension on the line. Tug, tug.
Where's my fish egg? Tug, tug, tug.
I spin around.
My little brother's hands
hide his face. I want to drop
my fishing pole.
I'll be in trouble for not putting my rod
away.
I try to wind the crank to bring the line in.
He screams
more. I drop
the pole and line
on to the planks
of the pier.
The sky is Utah blue and trees glisten
in the summer breeze.
The lake is empty,
all ours.
This is paradise. She's in
the trailer laughing
about her secret messages
and we're somewhere
other than, "in your own back yard."
There's only the two of us
to play
together.
There only ever is.
But we dig holes
to China
and set up Matchbox car

cities in the dirt.
We even have our own mulberry tree
to climb.
But fishing is so much more important
than digging to meet
Chinese children.
Our Uncle is a real fisherman
has his own boat, "The Lady."
He brought me a swordfish once
and cut off the sword
for me to play with.
When we visit Great Grandma Mimi,
his bedroom has big tanks with loud bubblers
for the fish he catches.
My mother says
he's not saved, so fishing must be
a dangerous job.

I kneel beside my crying brother,
my red and white float bounces
on his jacket
as he sobs.
I follow the line up to the pink fish egg
at the edge of his eye.
My hook is threaded
through his eye lid.
A trickle of blood runs
from the exit point.
Red skin is torn
at the entry point.
He rocks on the wooden dock.
Our dad flips open
a blade from his Swiss Army knife.
In one swipe he frees
my brother's eye from the line
to my rod.
But the hook is still imbedded
in his eyelid.
My heart pounds.
His cries cut through the crisp
morning air. His fishing pole with hook

pushed into the cork handle,
lies beside him.
My father picks him up
and carries him
to the camper.
I know what our mother is going
to say.
He *can't* be "accident prone,"
I
did
this.
My pole.
My hook.
My pink fish egg.
My
fault.
They take him to another hospital.
This stay is short.
No Gamma Goblin shots,
no ICU,
no Staph infection,
no Thrush.
In a clip of metal
and a couple stitches
he's released.

I show him how to poke his hook
through a bright pink egg.

Bebe

The beige paint bubbled and chipped on the bar
holding the forest green Naugahyde in place.
The kids on the short route got the new bus.
I didn't care, my best friend was on *this* bus.
At railroad tracks when the roof lights came on
the driver said, "Quiet all,"
opened the door to check, we stopped talking
and continued our jokes in sign language.
I wasn't allowed to play with kids on my street
so I didn't know.
Bebe seemed to know.
She was the youngest of seven.
Maybe she knew, knew my mornings were hell.
Knew getting me off to school interrupted my mom
drawing cartoons of the secret messages from
the General Conference in Washington DC,
appointed to decipher their underground messages,
the ones they snuck into worldly novels,
forbidden movies
and TV shows like *Bewitched*.
"Kids couldn't understand," she'd say.
It was an important job.
Making me lumpy Cream of Wheat
interrupted her secret work.
If the whack of the wooden spoon
at the table didn't make her point,
her bone-crushing hand squeeze
to tell me to pray by the front door, did.
I cried all the way to the bus stop.
Bebe knew.
I sat down on the cracked naugahyde
and she spider-whispered her fingers
in the hairs on the back of my neck.
My heart stopped racing.
My eyes focused.

The crane stopped our bus in slow motion,
smooshing the metal corner of the ceiling toward me.
The slow steel screech caught up on a delayed soundtrack.

Her face hit the beige bar.
Blood splattered across the B's and L's
of our Dots and Boxes game.
I don't know when the ambulance siren stopped.
Her doctor dad drove back to the wounded bus
and picked her teeth up off the floor
and dropped them into a carton of milk.
The brace encouraging her front teeth to take root
looked like a shiny chrysalis.
She chewed little bites of my 10th birthday
cake with her back teeth.
I knew.
I reached over,
and light as butterfly wings,
tickled the hairs on the back of her neck.

Black and White and Read All Over

I've been trained to pretend
not to see,
but my shocked eyes disobey
and stare.
There's crushed newsprint
on the green shag carpet,
the newsprint that delivers
her secret topsy-turvy
messages.
The newsprint we are forbidden
to read.
Yesterday's
newsprint is covered
in blood.
Boy's white briefs lay under the tapestry chair
made in my great-grandfather's factory
before the public offering.
I'm deaf to the morning hymns
playing from the Grundig Majestic Console.
Last night's screams
blast my ears.
"The wages of sin
is death!" she screamed.
Maybe this time
she really
did it.
A sin was bearing false witness
or any white lie, not honoring
our father and mother, which meant
immediate obedience to any long string
of commands
at any time.
Once I was beaten for breaking
the "thou shalt not kill" one
for examining the next-door neighbor kid's squirt gun.

His pajama bottoms are wadded up
against the sliding glass door.
Of the four sets of eyes framed in the family picture,

my brother's
are vacant.
A crushed tiny fistful of newspaper
peeks from under the sofa, evidence
of a futile attempt
at escape.
"Whatsoever thy hand findeth
to do,
do it
with all thy might."
Maybe this time
her hand had obeyed that scripture
to the letter.
I startle
when my mother shouts,
"Get your brother up for breakfast."

The escalating voices
and inevitable pleas for mercy
followed by
the sounds of a scrawny boy being beaten
by an obese woman
happened just about
every night.
But last night
she made him bleed
all over the paper, or maybe
she incited our father to participate.
She could do that by demanding he perform
his duties as head of the household
as commanded by the Bible,
if that didn't move him to action,
screaming that he was going to give her cervical cancer
with his uncircumcised "peus"
usually did the trick.
Even a father's natural protective nature
can be eroded
by enough
insults about his dick.
But whether one or both of them beat him
last night

the blood was evidence
his frail flesh was the target
of her rage.

"Lois!" her voice rings from the kitchen.
"Did you hear me?"
"Yes."
"Yes what?"
"Yes, Mother Dear," I mutter.
My 12-year-old mind races
for answers. The blood clots
she made us look at in her toilet
every month
to show why we all needed
to wait on her for a few days,
was her own
blood.
This was my brother's,
I was sure of it.
I remember a call from the school. Two boys
were teasing Sally Gray
from my brother's class.
They were on the way to the playground
where the handrails were made of two-inch pipe.
Was my brother one of them?
Maybe he had just got caught
reading her *Mad* magazines
with the secret
religious words
just for her.
I walk into his room, doors aren't allowed
to be closed.
"You awake?" I whisper.
He pulls the covers over his head
and turns his back to me.
"What happened?" I tug
at his bedspread.
"Nothin'
leave me alone."
"You gotta get up, breakfast is ready."
The clanging sounds in the kitchen

verify this.
His shoes and socks lay on the floor. Every now
and then
a large truck made the floor tremble
a little
as it rolled by on the freeway.
"Not hungry," he says.
He barely ate anyway. She fed us different
food than she made
for herself.
We were given small portions
of barely edible food
the kind she determined was
"healthy."
Daddy was allowed a couple bowls of cereal
after our rationed dinners
or a ceramic bowl of peanut butter and honey
swirled together.
But the church's prophetess
wrote, inspired like the men
who wrote the Bible, that children
were not allowed anything
between meals,
we could only watch our father
eat his
envied treats.
Our stomachs growled lullabies
many nights.

"Come on you gotta get up," I beg.
"Got a stomach ache," he says.
This might work.
She might not want him to go to school
with open wounds for teachers to see.
He might be able to stay
in bed
with a stomach ache.
"What happened?" I ask again.
"Gary lifted up Sally's skirt.
Mother thinks I did it."
"Oh," is all I say.

I go back to the kitchen and sit
at the table. In front of me
is one half of a broiled grapefruit.
My stomach roils. I feel
my knee-high socks slipping
down.
I say grace. "Our loving heavenly father…" I continue
saying words, but my thoughts
are jarred by the question
of what kind of god would make these rules?
I wasn't grateful for broiled grapefruit.
Our home wasn't kept safe last night.
Her screams of, "Wages of sin is death,"
punctuated by sharp blows
drown out my thoughts
and make me say,
"amen,"
unaware of where I am
in my prayer.
I feel guilty for being glad
it wasn't me.
The woman who was molested
by the same uncle
that molested and raped her own mother
from the time she was nine,
set a glass of milk
in front of me.
"Drink this,"
she said.
I knew the thick white liquid
was five days past
its expiration date.
I prayed she would go look in
on my brother
so I could pour it down the sink
and run a little water after it,
but she watched me
from behind
while making a peanut butter
and margarine sandwich

with a soft apple
for my lunch.
I hoped my friends would have something
good to share.
She wouldn't feed us any sugar, but we knew
that in the second drawer of the china cabinet
she kept a stash of candy.
Maybe he would have a chance to get a piece
of it today.
At last she left
and I heard the crumple of newspaper
in the living room.
The sour milk
and acid of cooked grapefruit
made my own stomach hurt.
But the thought of leaving him home
with her
today
made it hurt more.

Friday Evening Vespers

"You little imp!"
That was Seventh-Day Adventist
for "You fucking little cunt!"

Her nails flailed at my face.
I reached out and grabbed each of her thin
wrists with my hands.
The walls of my childhood kitchen
shrunk in around us.
This was the biggest family taboo.
I was defending myself
against her.
My mother
with starched black hair
piled on top
of her head,
her wild green eyes furious
and glaring I hadn't met the deadline
of reorganizing the drawers
she had dumped on the floor
before Sabbath.
The smell of frying veggie burgers
with melting American cheese
filled the air.
The *Review and Herald* on the floor
was open to the page showing Friday night
sundown was exactly
five minutes ago.
Her huge breasts jostled
under the Hawaiian print muumuu.
A red plastic record adaptor for 45s
of children's Bible stories,
sat under the console
as it piped out Sabbath hymns.
Her sharp nails were inches
from my face,
but now I was taller than her
and my grip was more
than physical.

Her body relaxed
as her screech assaulted my ears.
I let go.
My cheeks burned from inside
my arms from the outside.

"No more." I said it
this time.
I was no longer mute.
A few moments later I was confronted
by our house guest
for "man-handling"
my mother.
I held up
my scratched and bleeding
arms.
"This would have been
my face."
The silence
was the best
vesper hymn
ever.

Currency Exchange Rate

I rake the hairnet off my head.
His purple Hot Wheels dragster
rolls under the sofa.
Again.
We kneel after crushed hands every night to pray.
Whack. Red welts. Doors are never to be shut.
Hysterical cackles forbid children's laughter.
I stay silent.
Punishment for vacuum still on at 7:38.
Sundown.
Collect three tokens towards freedom.
"You have everything!"
Subtract two coupons.
Wear pants with flies in front.
Abomination.
Another token gone.
Give a child nothing she cries for.
"I'll give you something to cry for."
4.0 GPA. Add four trading cards.
Class president. Two points.
Baptism by immersion. Twenty-five coupons.
Bite my tongue that she dropped
out of high school at 16.
Choke down dinners with mold scraped off.
Six more merits.

Return the cross on a chain
to the bad boy in Canada.
Play hymns on the piano.
Stumble barefoot down the hall,
staggering, yanked by my hair.
Nine more coins in the bank. One for tithe.
"Yes Mother Dear," purchased seven more credits
for the privilege of sweating in this echoing
sudsy room.
98 pounds cling to rubber grips. Clench my teeth.
113 degrees.
Clutch vibrating handles to keep
the roaring machine from whirling me in circles.

Tongue-wagging sneakers grip at the slippery linoleum.
Over the floor stripper's thunder I strain
to catch approaching footsteps.
Concentrate. Remember it's safe here.
Focus on checker board squares.
Two round brushes spin towards each other, never colliding,
ripping last year's wax from the speckled tiles.
I grip wood over my head,
the shaggy mop strands plunge into grey soapy water,
baptized in tears, sweat and Pine Sol.
Thirty percent of minimum wage,
no check, applies to tuition ledger
at the self-supporting academy.
14 year-old virtual pay.
Electricity off at 10.
Up and dressed before it's back on.
Wind up the yellow smiley face alarm clock.
Sleep all night.
No arguing down the hall. There's a hall monitor.
Locked alarmed doors keep the desert valley
and pool
safe,
from us.

The lists of rules don't change.
Don't change.
Don't change.
Tater Tots, fries and mashed.
Three squares.
Don't change.
Upper bunk roommate attacks
with butcher knife stolen from cafeteria.
Towel racks rip from plaster. Still less violent than home.
I turned in every last voucher,
for the opportunity to survive this attack.
Odd days girls hike. Even, boys.
Daily chapel with segregated seats and cafeteria entrances.
But always the same doors. Same doors. Same doors.
No beatings. No belts. No threats.
Shovel cow shit for a forbidden electric skillet.
Bag twenty sacks of chicken turd for the contraband radio.

Scrub a crusty cooking pot, so big I can climb inside.
Stainless Steel womb of predictability.
Homesickness, an illness other kids get.
Steel Wool scrubs away memories
caked-on hopes of freedom.
A dish machine spews plastic racks of scratched glasses,
in a haze of screaming steam.
The vertical shelved conveyer,
with glowing hot coils for veins,
spits back its squared pungent
boarding school toast.
Overhead sprayer scalds. I aim and squeeze again.
Black floor mats squeak to keep me grounded.
Ravenous garbage disposal growls,
gulps my fear and grinds my guilt.
I wad my hairnet into a ball and punch
fuzzy blue time onto a card.
If I run I can make it to the factory line on time,
to box Schlage doorknobs for families
who believe in closed doors.
I can study by flashlight.
I can work longer.
I can stand the heat.
But I can't purchase the release of my brother
and his Hot Wheels.
Left behind to take twice his share.

Parking Ticket

I don't understand
what he's thinking.
I'm confused; maybe
I'm just stupid,
incompetent
or just plain unlovable.
He's helped move my boxes
to the storage unit.
He detailed my car
and picked me up
at the airport.
talked about the weather, what the kids
are doing and then he explodes
at the parking ticket
machine.
I want to run
away,
skip dinner.

Dramatic tantrums
or outbursts
of anger
in those close to me
have foreshadowed
their turning their rage
on me.
I've tried to hold
them off,
I've failed
at times.
I grabbed my mother's
wrists
when she clawed at my face.
I grabbed her
didn't let go.
She tore up
my arms,
but I saved
my face.

I didn't give that
up.
My first boyfriend knocked
me to the ground
with his fist.
I caught
myself
before my cheek skidded
across the asphalt.
My ex berated
me
until four in the morning
when at last
I curled up in a ball
sobbing in the corner.

But he only swore
at the parking meter
not at me.
Maybe he was just hangry
or needed a drink.
He needs a drink
by midafternoon
to be civil.
Maybe I'm reading too much
into this.
I stir
my ginger and wasabi
into the soy sauce.
I talk about my trip
to visit my daughter.
He changes
the subject
to my writing.
We pick up sushi
with pointed chopsticks.

I want to scream.

His Own Cartoon Book

Witnesses record through their own eyes.
My brother disappeared into the swampland.
The blonde blue eyed surfer
left California to be an Okie.
A xenophobe, homophobic security guard,
a massage therapist.
His Valentine's book
a witness to our childhood.
The bleak highlights:
catching our parents in the act,
the beatings,
all captured in his 6 point bio.
His disappearing act
his head bashed into door knobs
and wooden coat hangers broken over his body.
From the right of his star-chasing tail,
through the night sky
to a stationary
self-emulating speck
that disappears in daylight.

Dip

Our parents were buddies in the fifties.
Mine convinced his
to be baptized by immersion
in San Luis Obispo.
His mom couldn't conceive.
(Later she'd have an affair with my dad,
who said feminists couldn't climax either.)

When my mom announced
she was pregnant with me,
they adopted Randy.
After my parochial university expelled me,
I ran away to his room, since he'd moved out.
He invited me to bring in 1978
at the Peninsula dance,
to get-down funk and beautiful waves of black men.
Us two
white kids with no rhythm.
He wanted to dip me.
Halfway down,
I changed my mind,
afraid he'd let go.
Years later,
I visited,
the skeleton lying on our old bed,
six foot one,
90 pounds.
His mother left the room,
carrying adult diapers with blue gloves,
I'd been married at 21.
He'd complied with college
vaccinations requirements.
The sleeping HIV
thundered into full-blown AIDS.
Me, an excommunicated fundamentalist,
reborn into a secular world.
He, at peace with going back to dust,
no belief in eternal rewards.
All I could say was,

"Let go, it's okay."

Rearview Mirror

"Thank you," I say
to the private detective
as I hang up.
Real danger can only be assessed
though retrospect,
and a rearview mirror
is the only accurate looking glass.
I remember pulling the rusty
cab door closed
and reality grabbing
me as I tugged up
my muddy duck-print
panties
dragging from around one high
heel.
"Si, hotel Del Rey," I confirm
as Willie shoves crumpled pesos
through the driver's open
window.
Willie Rammer.
Later my therapist would
tell me
his name should have been
a warning.
But at eighteen
he was just the curly-headed friend
of my new boyfriend.
Curly and his flight-attendant
wife had flown
from the windy city to meet us
in Mazatlán.
This was only my second commercial flight.
The first was
to Sacramento
on an eighth grade school field trip,
where I declined the soda
for fear it wasn't really
complimentary.
Having escaped Seventh-Day Adventist

constraints, I only knew
my new boyfriend was
"of the world." He drank
Johnny Walker, smoked Benson
and Hedges and drove
a black Trans Am.
He took me to restaurants that served
courses,
and now had flown me to exotic Mexico
to meet up
with his boyhood friends.
The two young men took me
on a tour of bars with mismatched
chairs, seventies top 40 tunes
and shots of tequila with hash tracers.
I felt special,
grown up.
I laughed.
I danced.
This is what sin felt like.

When the battered cab dropped
me off,
I staggered through the lobby
and found a Pinol-scrubbed restroom
on the third floor.
I crawled across the polished stone
and hid between the toilet
and the wall unraveling into sobs
as I pulled at threads
from my blue
home-made skirt.
This was my fault.
This was what happened
to sinners.
In the morning he told me
he'd watched the whole thing
from across
the dark alley behind
the last bar.
The rape was set up

as a test.
A test,
which I of course
failed.
While everyone else sipped dark coffee,
I swam out to sea
hoping a shark or rip tide
would steal me
away
from the long silent humiliating flight
home.
But after an hour I turned
back toward the resort
afraid of what might be lurking
in the shallowing water
as I approached an outlying
island.
Guilt-ridden, I promised
not to tell Curly's wife in exchange
for a flight home.
With this incident my new boyfriend
purchased 15 years of control
and my acquiescence.
And now
the P.I., apologizing,
confirms the numbers
on the cell phone
did belong
to hookers.
Turns out he'd been paying
for it
all along.
I replace the phone
in the console,
turn up the radio
and press down
the accelerator.
The breakable bit in,
"Once I saw through a glass darkly
but now face to face,"
must have been

a rearview mirror.

Tape Recorder

I use a miniature tape recorder
to dictate patient notes
and psychological
testing reports.
I give
the little cartridges to a transcriptionist
who then returns them blank
and hands me APA-exquisite pages
to put in patient charts.
Today
it's for a different purpose.
I open the back door
to the Eldorado
(he developed a thing for these old people's cars
laying carpet for the Italian mob
in Chicago).
I press the play
and record
buttons
down together.
A little red light comes on
and I slip the device into the black leather
pocket behind the driver's seat.
Leaning inside
the Cadi,
I can see his cell phone,
plugged in,
the same one
I got the numbers from.
The P.I. said
Stress Busters and the Mirage Massage Parlor
had both recently been busted
by vice.
A U.S. Gypsum Corporation quarterly report
sits on the passenger's side floor
with a photo of a grey-haired man
and a VP smile.
Only his blue eyes were passed
down.

The "Kawasaki Lets the Good Times Roll"
lime green logo
shouts up
from the crumpled tee shirt
on the back seat.
A lone squashed Benson
and Hedges cigarette nestles
in the ash tray.
The leather still has that
new car smell.
I have to do this.
I need to know who Gina is
who drives the red convertible Mustang,
like the one he rented on our last vacation
to Sedona,
and who Kelly is,
who "can bring a friend along."

The P.I. wants me to be wrong,
but I know I'm right.

He leaves his Rolex at home when
he goes out
while I'm bathing the kids.
He's a show off, he never leaves
his Rolex.
The one I bought him
with the first money I made
as a therapist.
I need to know
what he's doing.
I need to know why
he threw me across the bed
after he came.
I need to know if having sex
with him
puts me or my kids
in danger.

Soon I'll read
the kids a bedtime book

about a boy who turns into a hawk,
and then sing them
to sleep.
He'll go out.

I close the car door
with Eldorado quiet
and slip back into
our home.

Scars

I've seen scars tattooed into fish bones
and ones tatted up with zipper pulls.
Men flaunt them
as card carrying warriors.
Women hide them under plastic surgery.
Keloids,
sloppy patch jobs
over original wounds.
Knotted speed bumps
that replace nubile flesh.
An inventory,
along with finger prints,
when arrested.
Petroglyphs
left by adolescents
releasing their pain.
My grandfather carried his,
sliced into his back
by his mother,
into an early grave.
Maybe scar tissue
is stronger
than the original skin.
Damaged dermis
bears witness anyway.
But the only time
it mattered at all,
was when my scars
fell in love
with yours.

Radio Frequency

She checks the boxes on her clipboard—
Postmenopausal: check
Two births: check
Abdominoplasty: check
Read HIPPA, informed consent,
limited liability: check
Labia to be reduced: check
Tightening: check.
He still dreams about the dead wife,
Young, two C-sections
vagina, virginal tight.
She still calls him pet names in his sleep.
I can't compete with death.
"Feet up in the stirrups, like a pelvic,"
the doctor says
in her Austrian accent.
RF is warm, not dick warm
but not speculum cold either.
I want to be tight,
suction tight,
so he has to pull hard to leave me.
"That'll be three treatments," the doctor says
painting my labia with the metallic magic wand.
"They charge 5600 in Newport Beach
at the inventor's stirrups," she says.
The tiny blue pill needs a pink pill bargain.
KY usher's the RF radiator up inside.
I picture puckering, sea anemone retreat,
a baby's arm holding an apple.
She says, "Can you believe these refugees?"
I see her eyes and nose
above the blue paper drape.
"They're babies and people being bombed
out of their homes," I say.
"Yeah, but really, what skills
do they bring?" she says. "I was a doctor!"
The dead wife fades into the sea of corpses
rolling out with the tide and washing up on the shore.
Give me your tired, your poor,

your slack post-birth pussies.
The blue paper rustles.
She lifts the stainless lamp
beside my golden doors.
Immigrants are foreign to the land
that invites them in.

Darwin Rolls His Eyes

Natural selection is the shadow I deny.
Forced at knife point, overpowered, craved.
Double helix puppeteer strings are invisible.
Grabbed, pulled by my hair, slapped.
They're the ignored ropes we all call "free will."
Tied down with restraints, pants cut to shreds from the crotch.
Tickets sell like hot cakes for roller coasters
to trigger my fight or flight response.
Blind folded, throat gripped, nipple twisted, gagged.
Netflix binging on sexual jealousy that engages my interloper rage.
Chef knife drawn across my chest, followed by hot drips of melted wax.
Blasts of road rage ignited by DNA, warning that disrespect
could lower social standing and so my chances of getting laid.
Claimed, owned, desired, without choice.
Choose chocolate over salad to store energy for the winter ahead.
Needed, driven, craved, objectified, helpless to resist.
Nucleic acid instincts command I obsess about my offspring,
who face dangers I don't even understand.
Ripped, ripped apart, ripped into, ripped from, ripped away.

Crystal Pier

Getaways are about drinking too much
where the kids can't see.
For me, hotel keys still hold a bit
of the forbidden and naughty.
Parking it in another zip code
gives me license to be someone else.
In the late 60s
the cottages built on this wooden pier
housed junkies, panhandlers and easy women
vacationing from the establishment.
I was waiting turns for playground swings then.
But Pacific Beach sold other flights.
At the height of the pier's debauchery in '77,
a mobster, "Bomp," was shot
in a phone booth down the street.
Since then the cabins have cleaned up their act,
and I don't use drugs unless I'm shot-gunned,
in restraints, with a hood, and the gag ball is removed.
When the waves break under our porch,
everything shakes,
or maybe the Veuve just kicked in.
I'm not sure what hippie versions of Silver Oak
and Amaroni were,
but the crashing of waves, jolting the wood pylons
must've given them sea-quakes too.
The pier's a sanctuary
leveling the field for grunts, students, and anarchists,
the have and have nots,
those wearing pukka shells, and flowers in their hair.
Now the gate is locked at sunset to fishermen,
joggers and lovers taking a stroll.
Out on the last cottage
at the end of the pier
a black and white seagull
eyes my nut-crusted baked brie.

Lies

Both our grandfathers were gangsters in LA.
We were born with blood on our hands.
The Packards and Tommy guns were lost
in estate sales before we were born.
Our granddaddies' adrenalin fixes orphaned
both our moms in Harlow's Rhesus lab.
Terrycloth maternal care, we both know how to pretend.
His wife died while inhaling and sipping at her addictions
during a Christmas party.
He says he wants to go quick like that.
I forgive his second Black Russian.
Aneurysm-fountain-of-youth smiles from the eight by ten
on the night stand next to the bed where I'm tied with red satin sashes.
I lie with a groan instead of a truthful sigh, when he pulls
the blindfold down, blocking out the photo of his fantasy death.
Later, sitting with my weight on the cheek with the least welts,
I ask about his A1C and HDL.
He lies and pours me more Silver Oak.
He asks if confessions on my couch paid the bills this week.
I lie and swirl the red nectar.
A crystal toast.
How sad that our bootleg-grandfathers were deprived of Napa wine.

Drum Beat

His river of grief
over becoming an orphan
in 3 months
carved out a canyon
of the loss
of the proximity
to his beautiful son
who moved to Tacoma
to be the creative director
for a gun company.
The orphaned father
picked up the drum set
packed it up
along with the music
and recording equipment
that his son left
in the bedroom.
Grief is a strange master.
She takes no hostages.
She slays every self-sufficient soul
strangling it with nostalgia
and a sharp knife of regret
all laid out
without a drum beat
in her wake.

Other People's Neighbors

Other people's neighbors
watch me arrive—
suitcase,
wine,
dog bed,
food bowls,
laptop,
books,
bicycle
and paddle gear.
The agoraphobic mother,
baby in arms,
screams
at their yelping Cocker Spaniel.
The boy, sequestered
in his garage,
shoots exploding soldiers,
while his grandmother hollers,
"turn off that porn,"
during our
Saturday afternoon delights.
Across the street
Sherwood Shutters
lives alone.
She'll be 92 in June.
Watches
from her second story window;
salutation kisses,
the start and finish
of our bike rides,
leaving dressed for dinner,
me shedding ocean-soaked
Dri-Fit
and him
rinsing out the sand,
me pushing
the arthritic hips
of my Greyhound,
while my lover bribes

him into my car
with fresh smoked lamb
when I leave.
A couple times a year
she meets him
out by her mailbox.
Sorting through donation requests
from her church
with a tremor.
She looks up and says,
"Reminds me of my first husband.
He traveled.
Was like dating
when he came home.
You're the most romantic couple.
You're doing it right."
Other people's neighbors.

Leaving

I've lived in this house for twenty-two years.
This is longer than any home I've ever had.
This house has been my refuge.
It tried to make me feel like a good mother.
I've changed it to fit me.
I don't know where to start.
I feel dizzy and confused.
All my things need to be given away or put into boxes.
All my family portraits are down for the open houses.
It's already someone else's house.
I don't know where I'm going to live.
I open a box of pictures.
We're still a family just thousands of miles apart.
I put a picture back out on the shelf.
I'll take it back down later.

L'Chaim

L'Chaim is the only Hebrew I can read.

We've been walking our dogs to Starbucks for almost five years now.

Still L'Chaim is the only Hebrew I can read. Not that she wouldn't love to teach me. It's what she does. Invited me to join her adult bat mitzvah class. But L'Chaim is the only Hebrew I can read.

Today I'm between residences, not homeless exactly. She offered me sanctuary in her home. There's pictures of those mourning the destruction of her sanctuary. L'Chaim is the only Hebrew I can read.

For ten days I'm alone with the dogs in the cantor's home surrounded by icons and letters I don't understand. L'Chaim is the only Hebrew I can read. Prayers and son's bar mitzvah pictures decorate the walls.

I pick out L'Chaim, it's the only Hebrew I can read.

It's peaceful and beautiful here, sparkling pool, fruit trees and lovely gardens, all a toast to life.

L'Chaim is the only Hebrew I can read. But as the days go by and I sleep off the franticness of packing and house hunting, a soothing calm washes over me.

The piano, menorahs, stars of David, depictions of Jerusalem, guitars, prayer shawls and kippas, still, L'Chaim is the only Hebrew I can read.

I've only known the vivaciousness of crowded Passover tables here, engagement parties, and Chanukah celebrations. Now it's silent, just me and the dogs. L'Chaim is the only Hebrew I can read.

But in the solitary contemplation of generous hospitality as I house sit this clergy's home, L'Chaim is a good thing to be able to read.

Dulcinea

The last time my local police department called me
in the middle of the night
I pulled on sweats and met
the patrol car
at a little park with basketball courts
and cement restrooms.
Restrooms my daughter,
who had been fourteen for only thirty-six hours,
had asked those boys
to stop and use.
She snuck out of the house
was driving around
and had to pee.
Those clean-cut Eddie Haskell types,
a mother's bane.
These two Mormon boys,
their mission papers issued,
slurping up the last drops of Coca-Cola
from a Sonic cup.

I point with a steel finger
at my car.
The blonde Sonic cup sulks
to the once-cherished shot-gun seat.

That cop must've had a mother
of his own.
He let me climb in the back seat
of the blonde buzz-cuts' car,
soon to be on blocks for two years,
and scream like a banshee
at the scared shitless Bible canvassers.

But now I don't have any children at home.

I'm not used to thinking of this police station
as *my* police station.
My home still seems somewhere else
with towering eucalyptus trees and a frog

croaking for the sound track.
But here I am
in a miniature version of my home
with a tiny replica of my yard.

"You found her where?
Oh my god
she crossed 6 lanes
to get
over there!"

Now Ralphs trucks,
Metrolink trains
and horns aimed at texters
are my background track.
My cell phone plays some elevator music
through the tiny speaker.
I look out the sliding glass door
at familiar wicker furniture.
I pick at potting soil under
my nails.
The red cap
of a realtor's pen
stares up at me from the tile
counter.

"Yes, yes, I'm ready,
what's the address?
I'll be there in five."

At 6 AM I walk through the double glass doors
and stand staring at the overlapping hive
of bullet-proof Lexan.

A uniformed officer appears
from a long hallway
carrying a Styrofoam coffee cup.
"You Lois?"

The city insignia bears one word
rather than a two-word city name.

"Yes. Thank you."

I'm amazed at how well we can hear
each other through the thick
layers of clear plastic.
Dulcinea,
sans leash,
wags her tail
and trots out
behind the officer.
The look on her face says
she very much enjoyed her ride
in the police car
and all the individual attention
from the night shift.

"Good thing animal control's running late this morning."

"Yeah, good thing." I slip
a pull-collar over her head.
Five days into my new residence
I'm already
on a first name basis
with the police.
Woman's
best
friend.

Shacking Up or Two Stacks

"So, will you talk to her?"
my boyfriend asks
again.
He reaches a hand toward mine.
I pull
away.
Sure,
why not.
We'll form a club,
the subsequent girlfriends
of the past husbands
of the Hayword twins.
I'll explain,
"Yeah most men want unencumbered sex,
but the past husbands
of the Hayword twins
can only stand intimacy
with a few zip codes
in between.
Closeness means getting to park in the driveway
and not on the street
like casual friends have to."
I'll advise her to invest
in a good overnight bag, because after a decade
of schlepping clothes and makeup
back and forth
I'm still not allowed
to keep any personal items
at his house.
Like he's expecting *his* twin to come back
home any day.
I swirl my wine
and take a sip.
Some things get better with age.
At least *her* boyfriend will remember
the aging Hayword girl
who asked him for a divorce
last Thanksgiving.
That a woman can compete with.

The photo of her identical twin
on my boyfriend's wall looks
like she did 22 years ago,
just before she died of a brain aneurism
at their Christmas party.
I have no advice for the brother-in-law's new girlfriend.
Every other weekend I plop
my overnight bag down
beside the locked cedar chest
at the end of
his bed.
It holds her remaining
personal affects.
I went through it once.
Read her diaries,
tucked under the blue dress
and all her desk clutter from work.
Poor grammar.
She drank and smoked a lot,
through both pregnancies.
I doubt we would've hung out.
I don't think he ever read
the diaries cover to cover.
He seems to believe
she was perfect.
The instant canonizing
of the dead,
for fuck sake!
At least the brother-in-law's new girlfriend
has Facebook-proof
that the surviving Hayworth wasn't keeping
her legs closed.
The twins' birthday is February 3.
Super Bowl
is an excuse
for my widowed boyfriend
to throw
a frozen-in-time birthday party
every year.
The only football fans allowed to come
are the still-married neighbors from Modena Street

where they all lived
more than two decades
ago.
He told me that the marrieds
had to vote on my admission to the party.
He warned,
it had to be unanimous.
At first
it felt like joining a secret society
one with Roman numerals.
But over the years, between writing names
in squares,
I've taken first quarter
and half-time polls.
After that
the crowd is too inebriated to conclude
any valid research results.
Each spouse gave me the same
quizzical look and said,
"Oh yeah, he's the only one
that takes that stuff
seriously."
So around Groundhog Day,
every year
I endure the repeat
high school reunion
of the dead twin.
I guess I could let the new girlfriend know
the Hayworth girls' parties just appear
exclusive.
BYOB.
A lot of B!
I shake my head and ask,
"What does he want me to talk to her about?"
I can tell by his big blue-eyed stare
that he's serious.
It's not a, you're-a-shrink kind
of will-you-talk to-someone.
It's something else.
"They've decided to keep
separate households," he says.

"He wants you to talk to her about how we
do it."
How we do it.
Well we haven't done it on top
of the cedar chest.
The rusted Ethan Allen pulls might not be strong
enough for restraints.
I blink
and pour more wine.
I didn't remind him that just last week
he told me his oldest son,
the one who was 7
when his mom died,
saved up for a pet deposit
at his apartment.
But five months later
he still hasn't gone back to the shelter
and adopted the tabby
he picked out.
He thinks his son may be afraid
to live with something
that might die
and leave him
again.
I'd call it projection,
but I'm off the clock.

This was the first Christmas Eve
he didn't spend a week
cooking his six courses
with pilgrimaged ingredients
for the dead twin's raggle-taggle
relatives.
The ones who hock garage sale finds
on eBay
for a living
and praise Jesus
while the twins' brother feels up
his two teenage daughters
crawling all over him
between courses.

No, this year
the living twin left her husband
for a high school boyfriend
so, no one made the effort
to keep pretending.
My boyfriend and I celebrated
with just our four kids.
After going *out* for dinner
we played
Cards Against Humanity 'til 2
in the morning.
That's how to do
Christmas Eve.
Maybe I'll tell her
if he can keep up with your kids
for hours of a raunchy card game
he's a keeper.
After all,
it takes a card from the black stack
and a card from the white stack
to make anything meaningful.
He reaches out again
and touches my hand.
My skin is electrified.
I think that's a better thing to tell her.
After all,
"'I drink to forget Stephen Hawking talking dirty'
won the first round
on the night of Jesus' birth"
might not be the thing to tell someone
I'm meeting for the first time.
I think I'll advise her,
"If you can't live without his touch,
live with it,
where ever
you live."

Photo

The bowling balls sound a lot like thunder
before they crash
into the pins.
I tap the air
motioning for the people
on the right
to crowd together
a bit.
I hold the camera up
to my eye.
I press
the button.
Everyone's squeezed together
under the bar sign
glowing green
as the third oldest of the sisters
holds a score card
over the shoulder of a niece
whose brunette hair almost
covers it.
One of the brothers
with receding hair makes
bunny ears behind
another sister-in-law.
The father,
still wearing rented bowling shoes,
holds the neck of a Coors
with an eighty-year-old
hand.
I no longer
hear the balls
rolling down wooden lanes.
The ADHD kid fidgets
with a bowling score card.
The mom's single black pearl necklace
is in perfect focus;
she's flanked by sisters in turquoise
blouses.
They're a team.

My stomach braids knots.
Another annual bowling party.
There was another S.O.
for a long time.
But this past year
the sister turned down his proposal
in Hawaii
so, it's just me
on this side.
I've been on this side
of the camera
for going on nine years
watching them smile
at the girlfriend
who's only allowed to look
in through this glass square.

Click.
My finger rises.
"Great one,"
I say.
The youngest sister asks,
"Did you get the 'Jack's' sign in?"
She means the one
over the entrance to the bar.
Jack is their father's
name.
The sheer mass of them
is still blocking
the worn carpeted entrance
to the bar.
"Yes," I say,
"I got everything in."

Cliffhanger

Cliffhangers are life and death
scenes in old movies.
A screaming woman lashed to train tracks
or pushing out a baby on a speeding subway
or the unknown outcome
of an adult child in recovery.
But it can also just be an outdoor sport defying gravity
clinging to a giant granite rock.

Today,
"cliffhanger" moved indoors
made of abstract plastic knobs and colorful
Carapace-like handholds
riveted to 50-foot walls.
A modern art museum
where I was allowed to touch.
Below the bolted Incredible Edibles,
I remembered like Gumby
how to tie a Pathfinder knot and thread the Belay.

"Do this right," the instructor warned,
"or he will fall to his death."
Giant fans whirled, blowing gusts
of air down the forged curving
canyons and crevices.
Human spiders hung from blue webs,
their ballet slippers curled around pink and green pebbles
protruding from the wall.

"Uh, I gave birth to him,"
I said.
"Think I'll keep him safe."
I hold up a perfect sailor knot
for inspection.

"Ahaar, a real pirate, ma'am."
And he gave the blue cord
attached to my harness
a hard yank.

My body lurched forward,
the seatbelt-like Belay locked.
The instructor said through a mischievous grin,
"Yep, you're set. Now one of you
head on up, head on up."
I have to look *up*
at my son now.
He's a grown man.
His cargo shorts bunched around his harness
He's tied the long umbilical cord through it.
His life line threaded
up,
up,
up,
through a pulley attached
to the speckled roof,
and descended back down
to my own black harness and
seatbelt stopping gizmo.
"Belay on?" he asked.
"Belay on," I said.
"Ready to climb?"
I parroted the words
I'd just learned.

Aerosmith blared
and the pink, green, yellow,
and purple holds lead the way
to the ceiling.
I pulled in the growing slack in the life line
between us.

"Ready," he said.
I scrambled to reel in the excess
cord as he scampered
up the wall.
My heart pounded.
His life was once again
in my hands
with the pleated blue cord
attached to each of our

bellies.

I have to do this right,
I thought,
it's important,
life or death
like a cliffhanger.
He looked over his shoulder
and called,
"Ready."
"Lean back,"
I said.
Hand over hand I let out the uncut umbilical cord
while he repelled down.
Then it was my turn
to trust the miniscule toeholds
to hold my weight.
I pushed off,
letting go of one hold,
hoping I could catch another
ridge by fingertip.
Then I was stuck.
There was nowhere else to go.
Even with a jump
I couldn't reach a single
melted Lego.
I looked down over my shoulder,
 "Okay,"
I said.
He could let me down
now.
"Nah,
you're not going to give up now,
look how close you are."
He stood way down there,
waiting like an echo
of my own words
when I taught him to walk
on a horizontal plane.

There was nothing else I could do.

I looked up
and around
for anything
I thought I could grab
if I pushed off with a toe.
I forced myself to clutch an impossible
tiny protrusion
of recycled material
stuck to the fake rock cliff.
In triumph I whooped
when I high-fived
the twinkling-starred ceiling.

"Okay, lean back,"
he said.
I knew he was smiling.
The rope tying us together glided
me back to the indoor/outdoor carpet.
I hugged him,
Now that I was a cliff hanger
maybe
I can be a mother.

Halloween

Halloween was the only holiday
I took off every year.
I was going to be a better mother.
Costumed as a belly dancer,
witch,
gypsy,
matching my daughter's.
Sacred rituals
were supposed to give children
security.
I conceived her
with clean ovum.
Hers have endured
numerous toxic chemicals.
Nine months
not one drop of alcohol
no pain meds
for her delivery.
I'm going to have
Samhain grandchildren.
A warning label,
Australia belly birth mark.
A stamp from wherever she was sent.

Tin Heart

Wood squeaks on wood
when I pull the drawer out.
Under the strap-on, fist-sized dildo
and purple nipple clamps,
I find two more wads of Reynolds wrap.
Black creases in the foil balls,
like the tarnished silver in my china cabinet.
I'd told her,
stuck waiting for a train to pass,
that if she lived with me
she couldn't work as a dominatrix.
She'd pouted,
like when she had to share a room
with three other girls
at a Rainbow Grand Assembly.
She'd worn a powder blue Jessica McClintock gown
with Sponge Bob bloomers underneath.
I thought she understood.
The drawer leaned down
on the sand-colored carpet.
At least there were condoms,
different sized squares
promising diverse pleasures.
I should be working on my parenting lecture
for the La Leche League conference
where I'm going to tell
all those parents
how the hell to raise
their little darlings.
Instead I crush
another charred chunk of foil
into the others.
There are enough whips, paddles,
and vibrators to stock a store.
Our housekeeper has folded
her bustier over the latex outfits.
A Dios, Maria's praying
for her mortal soul.
There's no more candles

to light in churches.
They've been burned empty
under the pipes.
My own mother told me yesterday
over the *Cinco de mayo* parrot
that kept falling into the garlic dip,
that it wasn't my fault,
then gave me details
of the government's imminent Sunday laws
that will send her
and other congregants
fleeing to the mountains
for their lives.
I bought a new valerian root tea today.
Maybe I'll drink less wine tonight.
Jesus drank wine,
made more
when he ran out.
I hear
he hung out with addicts
and whores.
My son,
in this Overstock suit and tie,
volunteered at the felony expungement
clinic at the crackheads-for-Jesus
church in San Bernardino.
My mother went bonkers
when he taught
his standing-room only atheist class
at Berkeley.
He won't talk to his sister,
she's never been
arrested.
I wonder
if I had a cardiac arrest
if it would make a difference.
I should have accepted
the pain meds for labor.
My heroism
has bought me jack shit.
The torn open Reynolds Wrap box sits

kitty-corner to a pink butt plug
under a bondage bar.
My knuckles turn white.
I squeeze together
all the pieces
of tin foil,
and ask Grandma Barbara,
may she rest in peace,
to forgive me
for wasting rationed goods
and slam down
the lid of the trash can.

Preening

I brush cigarette ash from the shoulder of her heavy pea coat.

"You can't preen me in this country!" My daughter snaps.

Tiny globs of blue gum across her bottom lip look like Smurf bites, residue from the stick of gum I gave her in lieu of a shower and real hygiene.

This meeting, if he's still willing to see her, could set her future. She spends two hours showering, shaving, sliding into dresses, and applying perfect makeup before "scenes" at fetish parties. She's so distant standing there three feet from me. This stranger, who grew inside me, came out and stared into my eyes as she nursed.

"Does she have a needle in her arm now?" My grandmother's wise words of four years ago ring in my ears. My daughter had been accepted to all 5 London universities she applied to after rehab stints checked her out of UCI.

I take a quick swipe at ear wax clinging to an earlobe. She recoils.

"Your boot strings need tying." I hop so I don't step on the bouncing straps flying in every direction.

She looks like she might hiss.

"That's not preening," I protest.

We duck in the back seat of a cab.

I strain at the cab driver's Caribbean/London rolled syllables. "Why'd you come to London for university?"

"It's far from home."

"Don't they have good colleges in California?"

"It's far from home," she repeats.

"Didn't they have the major you wanted in California?"

"London's far away from family."

I stare over at her phone. She points to the adult-child sex offender's paragraph. She's brushing up on research abstracts of the professor she's now 16 and a half minutes late for her interview with. I grip the sticky door handle as the cab clings to the left curb whizzing around stopped traffic. He slams on the brakes. Makes a 3, no 4-point turn, inches from the massive tires of a lorry.

Oh my god, not only is she late for her interview with the chair of the

Criminal Psychology department at University College (redundant if you ask me) but we're going to die before she gets her shit together!

The cabbie pulls up to a building older than anything but adobe in the U.S.

In front of the graduate department that's been awarded a million and a half pounds for research. She glares at me over her shoulder.

"Don't come in with me," she snarls.

"Oh. I'll just go for a walk."

The daffodils are blooming in the park across the street. Moss carpets the trunks of the bare trees. The wooden benches are pierced with brass plaques memorializing dead people. All parents still hoping their children will make something of themselves.

Slab City

I drive the six hours for my week-late Mother's Day gift. My son's soundtrack for our road trip starts with a podcast on venomous reptiles. We drive into the desert. He's brought K rations and bad-estrogen-producing water bottles, so I'm guessing a mimosa brunch isn't on the docket.

"Turn right at the next road," he says and looks back down and taps at his phone. Bombay Beach Club turns out to be a resort destination for the living dead. Even though the shoreline stretches as far as I can see and the water meets the sky like any other real sea, an unbroken line of dead bodies marks the high tide line, overlapping Tilapia fish in various stages of decay, their vacant eyes wishing me Happy Mother's Day. Crushed bird and fish bones pretend to be a white sandy beach.

It's silent. No bird sounds. No children splashing each other in the water. No motor boats racing. No wait staff to fetch me something stronger than a mimosa. Twisted salt-covered rebar are ghosts of a once star-studded resort, the sticky stench claims my clothing for Goodwill donations.

Nothing's green. Not a blade of grass, washed up seaweed, a tree or shrub, only gray death that hints at what the salty water has reclaimed. The ooze allows a glimpse of a beam from a once bustling restaurant.

To break the oppressive silence, or to muffle the moan of a zombie, my son plays a selection of hits from the 40s. He's brought me here for revenge for locking him out of his AOL account 15 years ago.

We drive past abandoned homes, all grey except for the graffiti. One says in big blue letters, "Bukowski Lives." I hope he's not reanimated.

The next podcast is on the history of the game of Monopoly, stolen from a nice Quaker lady, who knew? She didn't have an attorney for a son.

The roads are good for playing chicken with 50s or 60s cars. Anatomical hieroglyphics are spray-painted on the hovels. The desert is hot and empty. The post-apocalyptic get-away is a foreshadowing of what a real ocean will do one day. I shudder.

We drive out to Slab City, a community of hermits living on an old bombing site in camo-netting-covered enclaves. My Lexus is in one cross hair after another as we drive to the top of the "art gallery." Rebel flags, barbed wire and hand-drawn cardboard signs discourage my asking to borrow a cup of flour. This is the anti-OC with found art sculptures reaching toward the Mojave sky with their last hospice breath. A wind chime of beer cans and whippets chatters in the hot breeze. We haven't seen another human, only their attempts at statements, Vesuvius artifacts proving we've been the same forever, always being reclaimed by Mother Nature. The Mother's Day a mother deserves.

Never Brought It Up

My daughter thanked me
for never bringing
it up.
It was all
my mother
spoke of.
I played with Barbies
on the floors
of TOPS, OA and Weight Watcher's.
At twelve,
she showed me
how to throw up
in the stall
at the Chinese restaurant.
My friends' daughters
stayed
on the streets
on purpose.
On speed, the new
belted jiggling machine.
I shrunk to threats of divorce
over seven pounds,
at pig calls
over an extra five.
Soooooeeeeee!
The scale,
my magic eight ball,
predicted how
my day would go.
Studied for GRE's
on an apple a day
and an oatmeal bar.
Counted every hated calorie.
Bragged size two.
Twenty-four inch waist.
Diluted good wine
with soda water.
Solid food on days
that began with "S"

Slim Fast for all the others.
Nine-month famish
back down
to a hundred and ten
after each birth.
Tiny was the only safety.
 Of course, I never
brought it up.
A woman isn't more
by being less.

Trick or Treat

Latex dresses
vacuum seal
in her naiveté.
Stilettos for stomping
on paying patrons.
Six-foot whips to whirly-bird
her invisible shield.
The pin up girls
on the front of the flying fortresses
that Grandpa,
a B17 pilot flew,
had her blonde hairstyle.
Even her drug of choice
borrowed from the Beat poets.
I don't celebrate anymore.
Lights are off in my house
by dusk.
I don't want to drop paper-wrapped
corn syrup treats
into pillow cases.
Those little costumed tricks
that hide pranks
until puberty.
Sitting on my office floor,
the child of Christian parents
places a Jack-O-Lantern
in my sand tray.
We are both working tonight.

Fearless

I watch your eyes track the posters
on the wall of the underground.
They do that nystagmus thing
the way they did
when I held you to my breast
for the first time.
Like you are trying to focus,
but so much is happening,
so much to take in,
try to make sense of.
Then you latched on
and your eyes closed.
Now you sign the letters
of the words
racing in your head.
I try to read the words
expressed by your body
but they are your own
rendition.
This trip our roles
have changed.
You are the one familiar
with the terrain.
I am the stranger.
You teach me what words mean
like, "alight" for "get off,"
"proper" for "decent,"
"lovely" for "awesome,"
and even "aubergine" for "eggplant."
You teach me how to share,
share a hostel room
with five other people.
How to take turns
on a roundabout
in downtown Milan
in 5:00 PM traffic.
You teach me to trust,
trust people
with different clothes,

languages,
smells
and colors.
You model trying
new things,
practice saying words
over and over
until they come out
like they're supposed to sound.
You're fearless,
flips and sweats
where everyone else is dressed
for high fashion shopping.
You wear woman's sizes
when everyone else
is in child-sizes.
How to break out in laughter,
share a table
with strangers
and find a few words in common,
enough to smile
make a toast,
and maybe become
Facebook friends.
You show me how to ask
for what I want.
How to speak up
to a gondolier
for pick up
at our canal-side table
or entrance to your university
with a smile-pass
for your mother's admission.
The belief that you'll figure it out
with a partial address
and train transfers
to the teppanyaki restaurant
in the heart of London
where they set your ice cream
on fire.
You demonstrate that it's what's inside

that counts
while wearing three-day old jeans
and hiking boots
in fine dining establishments.
You show me,
guide me
and have patience with me
over six boat trips,
two plane flights,
two crazy taxi rides,
innumerable train connections
and 1000 miles of driving
a subcompact manual transmission.
Thank you,
my teacher,
navagatrix,
and daughter.

Granddaughter

I admire your audacity.
My father admired mine.
I wonder what he would have thought
of you.
Outrageous,
smart,
quick,
resourceful,
fearless.
He was Spectrum "painfully shy."
He said this about himself
many times.
I took him to a private magic club
once.
He loved to perform sleight of hand.
I thought he would climb out of his skin,
picking at bites
of the fine dining.
He let my mother dictate how everything should be.
No one dictates anything to you.
You stand with your feet apart,
melded to the floor,
and scold the Polish man with a cockney accent
for drinking our cheap wine
while we toured Italy.
You smile
but your tone says,
"This won't happen again."
I smile,
preemptive,
there are now two expensive bottles hidden
under your bed,
our bed.
I'm on the top bunk.
My father never stood his ground.
He was always vigilant
about where he was expected to move
and tried to anticipate what others wanted.
You watch for what's expected

and do the opposite.
I think it delights you to see people staring
at your bare toes
in the rain
or see shock on their faces
when you answer questions
about your major.
People remember you.
My father put effort into blending in.
Attracting attention was equivalent
to nuclear fallout.
He would be intrigued
watching you.
Alone though,
he could be fearless.
He gave us kids eyedroppers to suck up
mercury off the lab floor
after a machine broke,
spraying quicksilver over the linoleum squares.
He hiked us into desolate areas
and lived off what we carried in our back packs.
He would get stuck exploring dirt roads
in the family station wagon,
lock us in,
and hike out to go get help
long after dark.
He would've liked your uniqueness.
He would've understood your certainty
that you will always have a place to lay your head.
He would've got your self-sufficiency.
He kept his van stocked with provisions
for similar reasons.
I will have to be the one to tell you
he admires you.

Another Thing

"With this anxiety,
I can only get out of my car
at about half the meetings," she says.
A "One minute" chip hangs from her key chain.
Her makeup is perfect and her eyes are clear.
She's a grown woman.
But she still smells like my little girl.
Away for six months fighting demons.
I want to believe
she's slaughtered them all
at one of those seven hospitals and rehab centers.
"But that's good," I say. "Right?"
I swipe my 76 card for her pump
and then mine.
It's like she's dragging a corpse around.
Slows down everything
she tries to do.
Dead weight.
Dead dreams.
Dead as a doorknob higher power.
Dead ends and blind alleys
always leaving her
dead fucking last.
She squeezes the metal handle
and I hear gas pouring into her car.
"Enough for my court card
so I don't get kicked out
of my sober living house," she says.
She shares a room
with 3 of the 19 women in her house.
She never had that many girls in any grade
at the hippie dippy school
where she was a Butterfly,
a Spelunker,
and a Chameleon.
This is all my fault
just like my mother and my ex said.
I'm nauseous.
It's the gasoline.

There's a soggy lottery ticket on the asphalt.
My handle pops down.
The tank can't be full.
I squeeze with both hands.
"Fucker," I mumble.
"What?" she says.
"Nothing, just air backfilling," I say.
Her new sponsor
has eighteen years,
sort of.
She's a dry White Supremacist,
well at least into Norse mythology.
Gets into fights,
orders bad boys around.
Doesn't believe in promiscuity
or abortion.
But she's clean and sober.
She's working on a Ph.D. in psychology.
Hauls around a dual diagnosis too.
She's moving her ten year-old son
in with the latest skinhead.
She met him three months ago.
She and her NRA card want
behind the Orange Curtain,
out of the IE.
My daughter's tired of the little men
behind the Orange Curtain
and wants to go back
to London.
Back to the LGBTQ
BDSM scene
with an accent.
She's doing better at brushing her teeth.
"Did you pick up my prescription?" she says.
Her eyes are testimony
to the absence
of tablets, capsules, sublingual strips, needles and patches.
"We'll stop there next," I say.
My girlfriends rave
about her complexion,
weight loss

and new energy.
The men in my life
see something else.
Something dark.
Something lurking.
Something only men know.
Something wounded.
Something predators watch for.
Something yet to be addressed.
They refuse to speak to her
or ask her about her recovery.
They hide their helplessness in their resentment.
A drizzle of gasoline slides down the paint on my car.
I grab a squeegee out of the muck.
I don't want to see what they see.
The secret that stole her innocence.
The unspeakable taboo.
The thing that gave her a phobia of fish mouths.
The thing her aunties only spoke of in their fifties.
The thing that draws her to be pressed down and squished.
The thing that made her slam the book shut
when I read how babies are made.
The thing that skulks around her subconscious.
The thing that is only silenced
by needles
and prescription pads.
The thing that steals her,
her serenity,
and her beautiful voice.
Another thing I can't control.
I slam the little gas door closed.

Aspiration

At my office, the terrified caller
found a phone video of her teenager giving head.
Was sure it was her and her wife's fault.
Orange County's still voting on prop 8.
The Syrian mother, in a western dress
that revealed her limp (the price of escape)
speaks only Arabic to her five-year-old.
In an accented whisper, she told me
his teacher says the other kids are scared
when they play Power Rangers with him.
The mountain waiter repeated, "Gentlemen,"
with distain, to my trans kid and her dad.
She ran to the restroom in tears,
proud she could bounce.
The date-rape victim lied to me.
She won't make a police report on her way home.
I'd ask how many men might have raped her
at the party.
She was drugged. Out cold.
Hadn't considered the pain and bruises
could've been from more
than just her ex.
The soldier, trained with the US military,
10 years' active duty,
needs yet another psych eval,
to amend his application for citizenship.
ICE "lost" all his documentation.
His skin's too brown,
accent's too Latin.
Vet charged me $110 for doggy Advil.
Well, 70 of it was to rule out cirrhosis.
Closet drunk.
My brother's still radio silent.
Not fake news.
This Christmas my son unwrapped
two YUGE scrapbooks from Grandma.
I was 10 the last time she gave me something
that was less than a month
past its expiration date.

I got jealous when my lover shared a bottle of wine
with another woman, at his house, in the afternoon.
He got mad at my tears. He doesn't know
how good he is in bed.
I found the Roku remote,
the one I accused everyone of stealing,
at the bottom of my backpack.
My esthetician left a brownie on my desk, so I could sleep.
My lover bought me sunflower seeds
in a brown paper bag with the sides rolled down
to keep me awake.
Eighteen long months, living in a world gone crazy,
since my daughter aspirated her own blood
up inside a steel needle
before she shot up.

Day Pass

The Preacher droned on
entertaining himself.
The lady next to me
smiled like she knew me.
I scooted toward my daughter
on the other side.
She wore the red prayer beads
I'd bought her at the bookstore
yesterday.
She'd picked up a used book of Apocrypha quotes too.
On the stage a guy with a drum did a Cherokee chant.
It wasn't church music.

They gave her a day pass.
She'd been there for 30 days now.
After this we were going to eat artichokes
on Cannery Row,
at a table
with no other patients.
She wouldn't have to wash the dishes.

Her head bobbed.
I heard a joke once
about sleeping in church.
I listened without understanding.
I was always waiting on hold.
Her jaw was slack.
Her head nodded forward.
I read the back of an offering envelope
with a picture of Lakshmi
spinning something.
My daughter made a little snoring noise.
I reached up
and rubbed her neck
her eyelids lifted
a crack.
They focused on something
outside the window.
Before it had pews

this white building was a real estate office.
The two big screens were in color.
My daughter sat still.
A yellow pencil from the back of the pew
lay next to her flip-flops.
Her smooth fingers weren't spelling
the last word of each sentence.
Her knee,
inside her black tights,
wasn't bouncing.
Her breathing didn't move her chest.
I massaged her leg.
"Have some more ice water,"
I whispered.
She lifted her purple water bottle
the air whistled in as she chugged.
When the ice clanked against the plastic,
the woman next to me rubbernecked.
In family intensive
yesterday
I talked about how things might be
at home.
We got 90 extra minutes alone
with the therapist.
I had lots to say.
Three psychiatrists,
two nurse practitioners,
one GP
and an RN
all said Suboxin
couldn't get her high.
It could save her life
they all said.
It has an agonist and antagonist,
they all said.
I took lots of notes
on what they all said.
"Please don't be mad,"
she whispered.
She dozed off again.
Her water bottle dropped to the office building carpet

and rolled under our pew.

Unchained Predator

Once,
dressed in all white,
he cried
watching me
walk toward him.
Then I found out about
the brutal rapes.
Not all of them,
of course,
just of his two young sisters
and of his mentally-impaired
younger brother,
and mine,
a teenager drugged,
by the voyeur rapist.
The one he set up
in Mazatlán
and watched
from the end
of a dark alley
smelling of rotting
fish heads and used
tequila.
So today,
his estate attorney
called my nephew.
All the money from
business-raping
his best friend
into Job-like
poverty and divorce,
the 450,000 he raped from his
dying parents' trust,
the consummation funds
outlined in our
prophylactic prenup,
and all the revenue
from the sale of his franchises
and the house,

where he raped two decades
of bar flies,
was now liquidated.
Every. Last. Cent.
Tapping his phone
my nephew says,
"His attorney called to tell me
he's depressed."
I stop.
I look out the window.
Why bother.
My son can't prevent the inevitable.

I Step Down

from the slick step of the SUV
into the dark drizzle of 5 AM,
at that park.
That park where I would never
have allowed my children to play.
That park where families
don't spread out picnics.
That park where
they live.
Outlines of shadows blink
dim street lamp light.
"I'll count," I whisper in a hoarse voice.
"You ask the surveys?"
Three AM my alarm shook me awake
Last Saturday's training a decade ago.
We're given instructions.
Check bushes,
corners,
backsides of industrial buildings.
They meant homes.
He holds
McDonald's gift cards
and plastic bus passes
in his grown-up hand.
The same hand
that shakes incarcerated indigents'
as their young public defender,
mountains of harassing camping citations.
Headlights.
A car in the dawn
splashes down Harbor Blvd.
Glad we stopped
for hot coffee before our jaunt
around this park.
When had they had hot coffee?
"Have the flashlight?" my son asks.
He shines it on pages
of question marks.
Question marks that can't begin to ask.

I tally shopping carts
overflowing with
precious belongings.
I count cars with blanketed
cracked windows.
Tents buried under layers of canvases
keep out the rain.
We explore damp corners
burrows of human habitation.
Everything is asleep at 5 AM,
even in that park.
The round faced
slippered
Asian
woman
shuffles out
from nowhere,
rolled shoulders pushing
one rusty grocery cart
pulling another,
both covered with dew-splattered
blue tarps.
I tally: Woman,
Age: 40-50,
Street.
"May we ask
you a few questions?"
Her eyes narrow
staring straight ahead
gripping the bar of her cart.
"I have a gift for you."
He reaches out
a five dollar card.
"And another
after we're done."
She puts the brakes to her short train,
looks up at him.
I remember
reading him, *The Little Engine that Could*
at bed time.
I wonder

how much, "I think I can, I think I can,"
can really change
this situation.
"Census helps
secure funding for homeless programs
in Orange County,"
he explains.
shadows emerge
from the grey light
moving with
zombie-like curiosity.
"Do these yellow-button people really have free gifts?
They safe?
Can I circle around
be questioned again?"
"Rain wasn't why the police rounded up our friends last night!"
"The OC keeps its homeless hidden."
"I know a McDonald's serving breakfast
right now..."
The dawn peeks over
that park.
A mocking bird warbles
above a makeshift tent.
Bedraggled souls
step out
from a packed unmarked bus
dropping them off
leaving behind a cramped night on
Armory mats
into their daytime home.
"We have a gift
for you."
He says again,
before they shuffle off
to familiar corners of
that park.

Who's Crazy?

A Quality of Life Inventory.
A Minnesota Multifaceted Personality
and six of her cousins,
dots blotted out
plotted on a T score
crucified on a worker's comp cross
bleeding on to one date
of birth
life after another.
Relapsing,
legitimizing reliability
legitimizing validity
legitimizing there's no confidentiality
in forensic evals.
My son works
to send the insane to Metro,
better meds than prison,
but the test taker was a nurse
attacked by my son's saved.
Now they do calisthenics
on the back patio of my office
between coloring in dots on the tests.
It's a thin line
often blurred.

Another Rebel Heart

I open a book to the inside jacket and scan.
My son's taken up flying.
My daughter's almost 2 years clean.
I hired a babysitter for my dog's
unsteady hips.
My rectangular dragon boat paddle
and the pear-shaped outrigger one,
are locked in my trunk
at the airport.
Both teams medaled this weekend
without me.
But here I sit
on the scarred hardwood floor
of the upstairs poetry room
in City Lights.
The smell is one from my childhood,
Acres of Books in Long Beach.
"Can I help you find anything?"
the woman asks.

There's nothing to find
if I forget that I'm looking.
My son's heart is shattered by a six-year relationship.
My daughter's sewing hers back together without a needle.
My dog, Anubis, will soon arrive at the canine underworld.
The floor to ceiling books surround me
in this windowless room.
I want to absorb the courage
and creativity
of *all* its ghosts.
My own are bored with arthritis
and taxes.
As an ironing board,
my nose permanent pressed the smell of burnt dinners,
the smell of smoke in my thrift store clothes,
the smell of too much hate,
the smell of hiding,
the smell of superiority by virtue of the *right* religion,
the smell of Linkettes and Nuteena.

But, on those special outings
after visiting my great-grandmother, Mimi,
in Long Beach,
who carried with her the smell of liniment,
after that,
bliss.
Patina hardwood floors beneath rows of dusty books.
That was my real home,
the one where I grew up.
Where I towered above fundamentalism.
Where I found my head in the clouds.
Where I lost touch with reality.
Sitting here on the floor,
in my tennies and jeans,
I search for one word or maybe even a sentence.
I want those with rebel hearts to show me
how to make a difference.

My daughter loves Bukowski.
My son, Kerouac.
Anubis is still iconic.
And I've found someone who loves this room
as much as I do.

"No, thank you,"
I say to the clerk,
"I'm fine."

The Father

The father sat on my couch
his wide eyes
turning red a little on the bottom lids.
I had seen his first kid years ago.
I told him her anorexia and addictions
were worse.
Unfortunately, I was right.
She died in her car
in the parking lot of a mall.
He thinks I can predict the safety of his younger
daughter now.
The girl tells me she's a normal college student
experimenting
like any teenager.
The father looks at me expecting me to fix his pain.
I tell him I don't have a crystal ball.
The father and daughter leave my office.
I stare at my fish tank.
The frogs paddle to the surface for air.
They're amphibious.
I get living in two worlds.
When my frogs die I buy new ones for the kids to name.
I don't have replacements for my dead patients.

Juilliard

Our footsteps echo
through the late-night Lincoln Center
walking in the heart
of a sleeping Olympian.
Three blonde women
and one
with velvet ebony skin.
Her father's girlfriend
had been the first
to test positive.
Her mother never
threw him out.
We explored at a clip
after asking a lone valet
for directions to the iconic institution.
We centrifuged through the giant
glass door
and were flung onto the stairs
along rows of benches.
"I just wanted to see it," the black girl said.
She'd wanted to try real New York cheesecake,
see a rat in the subway,
and this, the stairway to young dreams
that led
to the blue Juilliard Bart Simpson
punishment wall.
A starched guard read at his desk
not noticing,
like she tried to do
when her mother gave her father
fistfuls of pills
in a trembling Libby's
until he couldn't anymore.
She started writing daisy petal poems
to not see
the box of small latex gloves
unopened,
unobtrusive,
unnecessary.

"You were at a Performing Arts High School,"
one blonde woman said.
"Right? Voice, right?"
I'd heard that voice
escaping its shattered container
deep inside her.
I didn't know it broke
her into a performing arts school.
The floor-to-ceiling revolving doors spat
us back out on the street
next to the number
on a headstone
for so many dreams.
"Yeah," the ebony one said.
"I just wanted to see where I'd be
if my mom hadn't died."

J.B.

They rescued him,
their cuckolded father,
from the bitch tyrant
who died 3 months ago.
The three daughters expected him
to dance with them,
to thank them,
to embrace them.
But no,
he sobbed for his beloved,
the touch of her
the site of her
the smell of her
the taste of her.
First the ischemic sadness burst vessels
into cerebrovascular grief.
Then colorectal carcinoma blocked his ability
to give a shit about what his kids thought.
His lungs filled with holy water
in an attempt to drown his sorrow.
But the morphine drip brought it all back.
The first time he saw the back of her legs
bending over
to release the heavy rubber
Mineralite ball
rumbling down a polished wood lane.
Yes, of course, he knew her flaws,
but the Beta-endorphin floods of make-up sex
smacked him back hard.
She needed him so much
it broke his heart.
So, the doctors fixed it
with a new bovine valve,
better than the ones he'd replaced
in those nitrogen hot rods.
But this goddamn one
anchored him to this pathetic world,
where he was a burden to his six kids.
The synthetic opiates fired up those

long-dormant dopamine race ways.
The ones that came to life watching her slip a bra strap
down a tanned shoulder.
He begged for his heart
to break now,
to shatter into a thousand shards,
to explode inside his chest,
to crush his breath,
just like it did back then,
when he fell in love,
once again,
so he can go
and be with her now.

Sons

I look into the sweet face of Trayvon
gazing up at me from the glossy tabloid
as I place the last can of Pedigree
on the conveyor belt.
The checker at Smart & Final
scans it with a hand tipped
by five colorful mosaics.
It's hard to imagine her sitting
still for these masterpieces
by the manicurist.
I wonder if these
are how she's rebelled
at what her mother told her
about beauty and practicality.
The gray-haired man behind me
in line places a six pack
of paper towels
on the moving black belt.
I remember teaching my son
how to count,
make change,
look both ways,
wait his turn
and hold the door for women.
The man begins rocking forward
and backwards,
his right knee locked,
stretching his leg out
in front of him.
I recognize the self-soothing
repetition from my intern days
teaching sign language
to autistic children.
I half expect his hand
to start flapping.
He doesn't smell
like grape gum
and milk cartons.
No, his unshowered,

late 40's body odor
precedes his rumpled
white shirt
as his rocking creeps
closer and closer
toward me
in the confined space.
I taught the autistic kids
to rub circles on their chests
with a fist
to say, "I'm sorry,"
when they hurt
each other.
It was my job
to teach my son
to say, "please" and "thank you"
at the grocery store,
yet not talk
to strangers.
My personal code is that I do not
educate anyone now
who isn't asking me
for advice.
It's how I stay
off the clock
when not at work,
stay fun at parties
and deal
with my codependent heritage.
At least that's what
I tell myself.
The smell of greasy hair fills
my nostrils
as I swipe my ATM card.
Staring at the floor he mutters,
"Nice day huh?"
in the directions of the cashier.
I wonder if his mother taught him
a few social phrases
to parrot for survival.
Mothers do that.

The urge to instruct him
on personal space
wells inside me.
But it's not my job,
I remind myself.
I look around him
back to the magazine rack.
So many things I never
had to teach
my own son.
I had it easy
as a mother.
My friends of color
must try to teach
life-saving lessons
ones I can barely find
words for.
I place the bag in my cart
and accept the receipt
handed to me
by glitter-sparkling
works of art.
I remind myself
it's not my job,
but the internal
conversation swirls;
"Sir, may I touch you?
Yes?
Okay take your arm,
that's right,
hold it out straight,
yes,
just like that.
That's how much personal space
is appropriate.
Like your mother
taught you,
right?
I'm sure you just
forgot."
No, today I walk out

of the air-conditioned store
into the heat
of the parking lot
carrying my dog food
and wonder
how mothers ever teach
enough
to keep
their sons safe.

Stubby

I left my boyfriend's home
and flew to Hawaii
to race canoes.
I invited him to come with me
to ogle bronze Samoans
and touch real Koa wood outriggers
but he stayed home to sit hospice
with my black arthritic greyhound,
a dog named after the god Anubis.
Now I'm not saying
my boyfriend is a saint
but instead of time in paradise
stirring Mai Tais with fruit salad sticks
and swimming with sea turtles
he barbecued Anubis
a $26 porterhouse,
with tears streaming down his face,
drove him to the Huntington Beach vet
and held him while he died.

That was my daughter's cue
to start pitching for a cat.
I like cats and all,
but with her out of rehab,
Anubis back in the Underworld,
my mother with her new Life Alert
I'm looking forward to more tropical paddle races
without anchors.
"I'll take care of him," she said.
"Pay for everything."
That had been true of the guy
she brought to Hawaii.
A cat weighed, what, 2%
of the skinny guy she hauled around
to family events?
My 3-bedroom house is too quiet now.
"Fine" I said.
After investigating seven no-kill shelters
she brought home

a long-haired
3 legged
cat.
Stubby.
He eats off my best china
in a pirate collar.
She pays for his allergy-safe
fish-free food.
Yesterday, I let him go outside with me
while I dug up dried tomato plants.
After all, he wasn't going far
gimping on three paws.
I brought him back inside
before she got off work.
Instead of topple, plop, plop,
rubbing against her leg
when she got home,
he yowled
at the sliding glass door.
She glared at me.
I shrugged.
She picked him up,
scratched under his chin.
"I know," she said.
"She gave you false hope
about what you can do.
I get it."

Loneliness

Loneliness is a powerful motivator in my life, more so than anger, disappointment, or even betrayal. Not being seen appears to be an intolerable state for me.

Loneliness in my first relationship overcame my fear that I would burn in hell for having more than one sexual partner in my life.

Loneliness eclipsed my financial fears and humiliation of breaking my wedding vows when I got divorced.

Loneliness creeps up and settles in like an evil possession. I fight it with work, writing, exercise, sending thank you cards, but it sneaks in and flows like bile thorough my veins.

I argue with it. "We're all one," "No one is an island," "Be your own best friend," but the clichés burst at the mere whiff of loneliness.

Loneliness immobilizes me, but also kicks my ass into motion. Strange drug.

I want to spin it into gold like Rumpelstiltskin's straw. Dead cells no longer needing sustenance woven into shimmering aliveness. Shafts of cut-off dead foliage transformed to something precious and desired.

Alchemy of loneliness, an artist's angst. I have to fill the hungry hole with something.

Moustakas writes of the existential angst of loneliness and how to embrace it. I think existentialists live in an existentially theoretical world.

In the last hours of labor with my daughter the nurse told me not to push, cervical swelling, but my entire body argued with her.

Embracing loneliness and not pushing on it, is like panting and resisting my body's urge to turn itself inside out through my birth canal. I don't know how long I can "just breathe."

Maybe loneliness settles in Eustachian tubes like a bad cold settles into your lungs.

To be seen is probably not a universal drive, just universal throughout my body and mind.

Loneliness doesn't bring flowers to my door, rather telegrams of the helplessness of invisibility that's my lot. Morning Glories rather than Stargazers. Glimpses not real connection.

In tribes we fought loneliness because humans are weak; we can only stand up to stronger animals in packs. Being alone is not only emotionally vulnerable but life-threatening in genetic memory.

My loneliness likes photo albums, yellowed stuck-together pages that rip pictures in half if you remove them. Portraits of another time, even digital ones posted with comments under them by strangers.

Loneliness settles down with a bottle of wine on a rainy day by the fire and looks through photo albums with me. We remember joyful bonds and memories with others, insinuating the hope of maybe more ahead.

I don't know what rest stop I picked up loneliness, but it's clear I now have a constant companion.

Pierced

plops to the plastic chair
just outside security.
She wipes the warm sticky
moisture off her hands
onto her expensive shredded jeans.
The TSA agent swiped inside her backpack
and over her upturned palms
with the brown wet tape.
They'd never detect the real bomb.
She was waiting back
in the US.
Heather replaces all her belongings
in her now certified explosive-free backpack
and reties her 20 eyelet Doc Martins.
The marque says one hour until boarding begins
for flight 431 to Oklahoma City.
She trudges to a plastic seat
in front of the countdown
to doom.
It's a cousin of the institutional chairs
in the hospital where they kept her
for 72 hours.
London had seemed a universe away
one year ago.
Now she's heading back.
Back to what her mom calls
home
and she calls hell.
She pulls at one of the rings poked
through her penciled-on eye brow.
It hadn't hurt,
not that bad.
Just made her tear up
a little.
She got the second one the day
the plastic stick showed a plus sign.
That one hurt.
She rolls one of the multi-faceted balls
on the rings between her fingers.

It's the same shape,
although miniature,
as the multi-faceted Christmas ornament
her dad
had used
to show her how a round earth could look flat
from where one stood
on its surface.
He would have understood.
Every sharp horizon is a precipice
to the end of the world.
But her dad was dead.
The cardiologist called it congestive heart failure.
Fancy doctor speak
for a broken heart.
That's when she got the third one.
The piercings are solid
memorials to those she's lost.
Violent attacks on her face
are permanent exhibits of grief.
The three dime-sized wire circles
bearing one, two and three black onyx beads
were also the last straw
for her mom.
The marque now says 15 minutes 'til boarding.
An ocean still separates her
from being a prodigal daughter.
She wants to run back through security
and back to the flat where Billy had held her
after they lost the baby.
But it's empty.
He's back on the street
poking holes in his own body.
She huddles under her hoodie
and yanks one loop from the puffy flesh
over her eye.
She slides it over her pinky.
She looks up to see if anyone is staring
at her.
All eyes are glued to phones and tablets.
She sits alone

under the ever-changing marque
at Heathrow airport.
She yanks the second one out
along with its two spinning beads.
How quick it is
to undo what took a week of obsessing
over the internet to find just
the right size ring,
just the right color stone beads,
just the right gage of wire,
just the right piercing parlor,
and just the right supportive friend.
Not to mention the tender care for weeks
of alcohol and saline.
She rips out the third ring,
and hiding her hand with her jacket,
lets all three fall to the floor
under her chair.
Jewelry is precious.
Even found treasures of plastic rings and bracelets
elicit squeals from bored little girls at airports.
But piercing jewelry
is hazmat.
Mothers warn small children not to touch.
Everyone will pretend not to notice
the three rings with onyx stones
until maintenance sweeps
them into a long handled dust pan.

Monarch

After the other butterflies
are set free,
the one with the broken wing stays
at the bottom of the white box.
The father of the bride,
a security guard,
took his gun and Taser to work,
forgetting this date.
He refused the plane ticket to fly from Oklahoma
since DFS hadn't made it out
to inspect his mobile home before the tornado
took it.
So now,
he's focused on protecting his next daughter,
the 12-year-old bisexual,
asked by stepdad
to watch her break her cherry
with a dildo.
The monarch fans its one good wing,
antennae searching for help
and possible danger.
Wearing a black Halloween wig scavenged
from a Goodwill costume bag,
a woman supports her full-body tremor,
damage from drugs and alcohol,
with a three-legged cane
tied with a mother-of-the-bride courage.
She didn't forget,
just said she wasn't coming
after spewing threats to call the police
on the bride
the day before
the wedding.

The monarch strains to stretch its tattered wing
in the salt air.
The bride's half-sister,
a FAS testament to their shared mother,
is dressed in full bridal attire.

Her white gown stands out against
the sand as she stares out at the ocean
wearing her mother's perfume,
diluted by the smells of the beach.
The other butterflies,
long gone on the late afternoon breeze,
left the wounded one
alone.
The minister asks the groom
if his family speaks Bulgarian.
Smiling,
he replies they speak Macedonian
in Macedonia.
I wonder how many stupid questions
he's been asked in his two weeks
in the U.S.
The six-year-old reaches into the box
lifting the injured butterfly
with a delicate hand.
The same small hand that zipped
up her mother's bridal gown
this morning.
A solution to a final quandary
the two of them have had to face
living on their own
for the past six years.
The bride's grandmother talks to herself,
spitting bits of food from a mouth
over-stuffed with beef ribs
and sour dough.
She plots to get her great-granddaughter
to come home with her
on the wedding night,
to teach her about
Jesus and the plagiarizing prophetess.
She and the bride's own mother construct
empty promises,
veiled threats,
the young prize to be won over,
bringing financial support
to whomever maneuvers to care

for her.
The child tries again to make the butterfly
fly.
It clings with tiny feet to her finger.
The groom,
in accented English,
repeats himself
as the bride's family speaks
to him as though he's deaf.
He graciously responds when the silent J
in the middle of his name
is pronounced,
like a brand of mustard.
The restaurant charges corkage fees
on the Martinelli's.
Children of Adventists missionaries pretend,
make toasts with pretend,
nonalcoholic cider.
It's all pretend.
The butterfly slows the opening and closing
of belabored wings.
The bride's cousin rakes up pink rose petals
from the sand.
Skype to Eastern Europe
is disconnected.
The horizon turns orange and red.
The six-year-old places the dead butterfly
under a bush.
Its broken wing glistens
with her tears.
The bride gathers up her bustle,
kneels down beside her daughter
and says,
"At the end it had
the best friend of its life.
It was the luckiest butterfly
in the whole world!"
The child wipes her face,
and with small moist hands
reaches up
for one of her mother's,

and the one offered
by her new step-dad.
Stepping from the chrysalis of waiting for visas
and navigating relatives,
they walk up the sandy stairs
to the reception
and into a life they create
together.

Off

"He wasn't trying to kill himself," she said. "It was to try to feel better. The cutting part anyway." She giggled and shifted her weight on the black leather couch. Heavy mascara eyelashes asked for my confirmation. Months ago I'd given her the brown sack of knives back. "The cap sleeves didn't hide it." She plucked something from between her teeth. "But I went anyway."

"Oh," I said.

My stepson called earlier. A text-based video game to demonstrate depression. For those who aren't depressed and can't imagine. The game creator was harassed because she's a girl. Her ex-boyfriend posted naked pictures. Blogged what her vagina smelled like. Threatened rape. Depression expert.

My stepson said playing the game gave him the courage to tell. To tell through his fog of 10 hour night shifts as a dispatcher for tankers. To tell that's the reason he drinks too much, gambles his vacation pay. To tell why he never takes time off. Isolation is portrayed in the game. The Depression Quest game. He used to play Ever Crack for days straight living on Pepsi. Now he wanted a cat. A kitten really. The Humane Society spayed and gave vaccinations.

The patient just before Mascara Eyes had said, "If Robin had only had enough faith in Jesus." Everyone wants to save the sad clown. No one's better at saving than a two thousand year old saving pro. The Jesus kid had beagle eyes and picked at his nails. Maybe Ork was waitlisted for a crucifixion.

Mascara Eyes swore by stigmata and white scars with hash tags.

At seven, humans understand death is permanent. Seven in human years not cat years.

I've lost some of those I've treated to a Co2 hose, a robe belt, starvation and overdose. There's no making sense of it. Ending the pain. Sacrificing. Avoiding a threatening future.

Mascara Eyes got stitched up at a doc-in-the-box after she called me and said she could see bone.

The Jesus kid found a fake family after rehabbing off meth.

My stepson calculated the cost of kitty litter and Cat Chow.

I clicked the mouse and started the next game level.

SanGria Whine

foil blister pack of Sam-e slices open

        my index finger

       crying unpronounceable Jamaica

One crimson teaspoon spreads asymmetric on

              the bleached table cloth

      Honey inherited curly hair grows out with flat sides

         climbing on bougainvillea vines towards the equator

Hoodia soaked contact lenses

           tears of jasmine night heir

When friends stay   hospice lottery   beats death to death

      Sun magnifying an ant into flames

Ajax-rough scrubbing vacuum cleaners and dialysis

      OCD chasing dust mites and wrinkled elephant memories

The owl in Pooh's corner hooted me, "you gotta play the team that gets off the bus."

Saline waves crash on the shore

      menses wash back out to sea

Drumming a woman's heart circle   Calling in   the powers of the east

     a Japanese PFLAG waving at women dancing

              backwards

               in heels

P.O.L.S.T.   garlic for poltergeist?

     Donate my corneas but put my uterus on the auction block

Have answers. will work for questions.

     ¿Por que?   Por que   Special K   It's okay

But the next letter, L, started an IV in ICU

    abandoned b_ood sucked upwards in a thin glass tube

    at the end of my finger

Menarche butterflies migrate in horizontal tornadoes

crushed on windshields of Mac trucks   transporting Marlboros

Deep-fried snowflakes served to homeless children using slide rules for Xbox 360 controls

YYUR--- too wise you are

Yogi takes the fork to eat Pooh's honey on easy street with Boo

While Sisyphus rolls silly putty over Sunday comics

My sanguine sangria whine

Hysterical Mimosa

I brought the OJ
from my own trees
in the same half gallon mason jar
that Conversion Disorder pregnancy girl
brought her OJ in
the night my son invited
her to our New Year's Eve
fondue party.
"You don't have to sit with her
while she pretends to miscarry," I said.
I'm not such a good mom.
I brought champagne
to go with the OJ
to the first women's team meeting
of the season.
I knew the co-captain was in recovery.
I didn't know her wife wanted a teatotaling
outrigger team.
I toast my Al-anon membership
with my mimosa,
"Here's to the things I cannot change,"
and then hide the champagne bottle
behind some cookie boxes
on a potluck table.
The attorney who strokes,
and brought mimosas
to the paddler's open house,
raises her orange bubbly plexiglass
from across the room.
Girls' teams have always mystified me
hysterical blindness
hysterical moods
hysterical ostracizing
the hysterical hysterics
and now
grandmother to hysterical pregnancy
and spiked orange juice.

Mirror Neurons

I have professionally trained
mirror neurons.
Put me behind
a great paddler
and voilá.
Sit me behind
a paddler who can't reach
and who tears through the water
and well,
neurons that fire together
wire together.
My performance pathways
have detours
hardwired
when shame
comes on board.
Scold me
berate me
even give me multiple directives
and detours fire
lighting up my
neuro highways.
No amount of reassuring
myself
that I'm not six
and a wooden coat hanger
isn't about
to break over my skin
will help.

Silver

Rough ocean
77°
49 canoes
on the starting line.
Another novice skipper
on his chase boat
with no ladder
for swimmers.
I hope he remembers
to turn off the propeller
when I'm in the water.
Change coach
sweet as a kindergarten teacher
with Oreos and fresh coconut.
Steersman hard-catching
for a first place.
Comedian in seat 3
joking about mermaids smoking seaweed.
Racing in the young adults division
rubbing Icy Hot
on my arthritis
to keep up.
The radio says
we're cleared for first changes.
The skipper revs
throwing up wakes
shuts off the engine.
I jump overboard
slap the water with my hand.
Steersman lines up
on my geyser.
No one mentioned
the circling fin
until we were putting life vests
back on to the trailer
wearing
our silver medals.

But a Dream

I don't row.
I paddle.
7, 8, hut, hike, ho.
I don't paddle my canoe.
Well, I don't paddle my *own* canoe.
7, 8, hut, hike, ho.
I'm one of six.
The canoe is the seventh member of our team.
7, 8, hut, hike, ho.
I explain this to my mother.
She's feeling better.
That green sparkle is back.
Still, she's forgotten my story
about last weekend's race,
28.3 miles of open sea.
The tea leaves stayed
duct-taped to the Menehune notch
on the back of outrigger number 19.
7, 8, hut, hike, ho.
Piemonte was the steersman.
I sat seat 5.
As we approached Avalon,
Tamara, seat 4,
kept taking her paddle out of the water
to look for a hole in the blade.
7, 8, hut, hike, ho.
"And 666 means love," my mother says,
"not the devil, like on tattoos."
"Oh," I say, "Hmm."
Her Amazon parrots screech over me.

"And there's a palm tree,
like they have all over the world,
at one gate," my mother says,
"and a lion,
like I draw, at the other."
I stare.
She pats her Bible.
"I'm going to make Ezekiel's secret clear,

so that anyone can understand."
"Uh huh," I say.
We'd been pulling hard for an hour and a half,
Now paddling down the last two miles.
Tamara stared out at the horizon,
dipping only the tip of her out-of-time paddle in the water.
Piemonte yelled.
7, 8, hut, hike, ho.
I shouted for her to follow
the wide orange jersey in seat 3
7, 8, hut, hike, ho.
But she'd faded back into her own world.
6, 7, 8, hut, hike, ho.
"Two boats," I said, under my breath,
"passed us as we approached the finish line."
My mother pulled her caricatures from a manila envelope,
lions, wombats, and palm trees.
"I'm the only one," she says, "who knows this."
"Alright," I said.
I count the sets of sixes,
in rows,
on each page.
My life is but a dream.

It Might not Matter

There's no room
under the seat
of a 6-man canoe.
I unzipped my splash skirt
with the green army man
crouched with his rifle
tied to the white pull,
and crawl under it.
I can't find the button
to turn on the pump.
It might be necessary
during the rough ten-mile
ocean race.
Position is everything.
My mom's position
on estate planning
is that she'll just go to sleep
and wake up when Jesus returns.
That he was named Joshua
the first time around
is an irrelevant detail,
and it still won't get her
a trust
or even a will
for that matter.
My son and I
tried to find
the right words
at the correct decibels
to make her understand.
Maybe it will matter
maybe it won't.
The steerswoman pokes
her steering blade
under the stern,
keeps us lined up
on the starting line.
I push anything
that might be an on button

above and around
the white cylinder
bungeed to the hull
of our boat.
This is no position
to start a race.
I'm a stowaway
not a seat five
engine room
paddler.

The air horn blares
I bang my head on the gunnel
the pump
hums
seat four swings me my paddle
over her shoulder
we're off with a chaotic
start.
I zip up the canvass skirt
with the little army-man pull.
At least
he's prepared to die.

Stand-Ins

Somewhere hiking
up in the mountains
beyond cell reception
are campers
oblivious to what they've left us
to face.
Our women's coach
left her second in command
and her wife,
in charge.
Our rec coach
passed his steering blade to
Attorney Asperger.
There's no way
they could have predicted
and couldn't have avoided it.
The steroid women
lost their tempers
tantrumed at each other
gave relentless directives
without a single compliment,
or maybe one
that sounded
just like a scolding.
Red Bulls in hand
they stomped off
the team.
No great loss
except for the theater.
We had to send out
rescue boats
for the trusting paddler
who inquired of Asperger
for a lesson in steering.
He sent her off alone
into the high winds
a swift current
in a 400 pound heavy.
"Sink or swim"

or be carried backwards
paddling and poking
with all her might
into the wildlife preserve
and out of sight.
When Moses descends Sinai
to the vista
of missed-placed veal
someone will drink
gold-speckled water
upon the coach's return.

Eight

At eight, the 8th grade girls
on the yellow school bus
tricked me into believing
I could become invisible.
"Hold your breath and close your eyes,"
they'd say.
I'd scoot my penny loafers
on the black walkway
bouncing between the Naugahyde benches.
The familiar diesel fumes filled my nose.
The air brakes pitched me forward.
I explored the air with my hands
and smiled with my almost-grown-in buck teeth.
"Where's Lois?" they'd say. "Where'd she go?"
That's the year I understood,
my mother could be tricked by men
with "Elder" in front of their names.
She stopped seeing reality at eight,
when she lost her own mother to cancer,
and became invisible at eight.

Home Scent

Dinner smells sucked up into
a clattering exhaust fan
covering angry stomps.
"So, what's for dinner?"
Bruises and welts
and tattletales
to Daddy,
who threw up
his own soft hands
to deflect airborne bicycles,
airborne shoes,
airborne blasts from the hose,
airborne fists,
airborne distain
on squealing tires
dragging Dad airborne
for the neighbors to watch.
The most enduring memory
is smell.
Not a pairing
or a correlative
but a trigger.
The soul of every home has one
that hints at its secrets—
soured milk,
diesel exhaust,
generic Windex,
Stripples,
Phisohex,
Dep hair gel,
drug store gardenia,
Old Spice,
cum soaked Kleenex,
Comet cleanser,
vinegar in her pink bathroom.
I've read that dogs can smell fear,
even the ones not housebroken,
beaten because they weren't taught.
Smell is the only sense

that requires an actual piece,
a sacrifice, a dismemberment,
to be recognized.
To remain intact
is to be scentless,
whole, complete,
original,
but undetectable.
Welch's at Eucharist,
Net Hairspray, a soft dollar bill,
and flat Shasta orange soda
disintegrated up my nose
into long-term storage.
She's 84 now.
Rotting garden vegetables,
Pomeranian pee
and moldy bird seed aromas
add to a long finish,
accented with metallic security door
with undertones of rust.
The yapping matted pack serves as her doorbell.
I breathe through my mouth.
Again.

Pubes

The orderly raked the adhesive
glove over the part he'd finished
shaving,
ripping the loose hairs up
with a Velcro sound.
"Ouch!" my mom said.
"The last time I was shaved
down there
I had your brother!"
Oh god,
they used to make family
members wait outside
the curtain
while they did this kind
of procedure.
"Well, maybe,"
I said,
"You'll come back from the OR
with a baby."
"Oh, no!" she said.
"You were too mean to your brother.
I never wanted another kid."
Maybe the 27 Filipinos
who waited with me in
the family waiting area
will adopt me.
I couldn't understand
a word they said,
but they seemed to like
my hair.
"I was bald and naked
when I came into this world,"
she said.
"And I'll go out that way."
The short orderly with stubby fingers
looked nervous.
The hospital smell overshadowed her
gardena cologne.
The green curtain

hanging by silver chains
was pulled half way around.
Her maroon outfit with accessories
was ziplocked
in a clear bag
on the floor.
An accordioned straw wrapper
was wedged under a black wheel
of her bed.
The orderly left.
"You're not going to die,"
I said.
The blood pressure monitor
beeped
192 in a red square
flashed over 98.
"I'm going to have a stroke
in there," she said.
A nurse turned off the
sound.
"You're going to be fine,"
I said.
"It's been fun
being crazy," she said.
"I laughed a lot.
I enjoyed myself immensely."
She smiles.
She likes that she's stumped me.
"Want more ice?"
I said.
I feed her a spoonful.
The doctor explains
they're going to snake a tube up
through her groin
into her heart
and shoot it full of a contrasting dye
and take pictures.
"I'll smile
for the camera," she said.
When the dye is injected
she mistakes the pain in her jaw

140

for a stroke.
They give her morphine
to calm her.
It stays in her system
all the way home.
In the car we pass
a strip mall
with the laundromat where I was dropped off
as a kid
every Sunday
to do the family laundry.
Until the day a flasher ripped off his shorts
and beat off
while I folded
my underwear.
"Know what my greatest regret is?"
She asks staring at the line of businesses.
"No, what?" I ask.
"Not buying the sterling silver flatware
I saw in that coin store
next to that laundry place."
"Oh," I say.
"What's your biggest?" she asks.
The green curtain.

Beep Beep

Her eighty-four-year-old hand taps open and closed
as if she were doing the chicken part of an Oktoberfest song.
I frown and shake my head.
I am sure she's never been to an Oktoberfest,
ever.
She sits on a black stool
perched inside a plexiglass rectangle.
The tech raises her hand high in the air
and brings it down fast.
"…and exhale," she says.
Her round cheeks collapse as she demonstrates.
With one hand on the tube she is blowing into,
my mom keeps beeping her thumb and fingers at me.
She's hyperventilating,
the pulmonary test is repeated again,
and once more.
Those green eyes want something.
She doesn't drink or dance
so I'm certain it's not "Chirp, chirp, chirp."
The pulmonary tech gives her an inhaler
and my mom sucks the fluid
in one labored breath at a time
"Then we'll repeat the test," the tech says
and closes the clear chamber door.
My mom points to my purse with her tapping hand.
A picture,
she fucking wants me to take her picture.
I take her picture—
sucking on the tube
inside the clear chamber.

Zeitgeist

I don't have a card.
I sit in the sweet smelling lobby.
Country music plays
with ballads of loss and shame.
Dispensary music;
he's getting me chocolate.
The place is packed.
He did time twice
for what is legal now.
There should be a word for that,
having paid severe consequences
for something that is now
every day normal,
ubiquitous,
legal.
Such as:
single women in bars,
same sex love,
interracial marriage and children.
marrying into a different religion,
not believing in God,
women in the military.
What prices are people paying today
for things that will be no big deal tomorrow?
We won't give them compensation
or say we as a culture were wrong.
We won't even have a word for this
short-sighted trauma.

Dead

It was the second "Celebration of Life,"
that euphemism of denial,
in three months.
The patriarch, following his wife of 65 years,
died of a broken heart.
All six kids and seven of the eight grandkids were there.
The eighth was still doing time for attempted murder.
"Can I help?" she asked.
Maybe no one heard. Their backs were to her
as the oldest rushed to get the food out.
The men kept hitting their heads on the long plexiglass vent
over the stove. Empty serving dishes with blue sticky notes
were arranged on the buffet table.
The sickening smell of steak and shrimp made my stomach turn.
Death and more death. Ingesting death to mourn death.
It would be the death of her.
The photo montage flipped through 87 years of pictures
on the sixty-inch TV, along with dead parents
there was a smattering of dead spouses
from 110 Kodak cartridges.
The dead are never dead
until the living stop using them as weapons.

Tides of Death

He picked 100 of his mother's favorite songs
for the memorial cruise.
His mother asked for a send-off
like the one he threw
for his wife.
Ashes to ashes,
float for a moment
then join the bed of sailors,
the conquered
and the mutineers.
Those who drowned
in the place
we came from.
Those who didn't make it
home to land.
The request of her son
was for bottomless mimosas
on the ocean,
but an open bar
would be a mistake
this tour.
The Hornblower will float the living
high above the waves.
Last weekend those waves
washed over my lap
soaking the gunnel
of my outrigger canoe,
I bailed
with a cut-off bleach bottle
to get my team
back in the race.
The hulied canoe behind us
left paddles and PFD's
scattered over the waves.
Bananas are forbidden
because they float
as a watery grave stones
after a canoe and its paddlers
sank.

The cold waves douse
our race momentum,
weighing down the boat.
I bail out scoops
of cold-water death,
rocking back-and-forth in time
with the other five paddlers.
Something of a mermaid siren
calls
us back to the sea floor.
Bring enough cash
for my bottomless mimosas.

Back

"I can't keep my Life Alert in my bra,"
my mother says,
to the checker at Michael's.
"It's too hot. I sweat."
I pay cash for the plastic packet
of 30 tiny key rings.
"I just wear a muumuu in the afternoons,"
she says
over the cashier
she can't hear.
I zip my wallet
and take her elbow.
"Let's go over here,"
I say,
and hook her Life Alert
to a black lanyard.
I slip it over
her starched hair.
Fallen three times
back collapsing down on itself
one crushed vertebra
into another
no feeling in her feet
one swollen leg
her home
an obstacle-course
Pomeranian potty pads
crumpled magazines
outdated papers
she shoves aside
with her three-pronged cane.
"Your doctor says…," I start
but it's no use,
she's talking again.
A light flashes
from one side of her chest.
"I have to turn it towards me,"
she says and digs on the side that had the cancer,
"or I have a blinking headlight."

She picks up the torn-open package.
"I'll put the rest of the rings
in my tool box,
for later."
Twenty-nine left-over rings
saved with her other treasures.
It wasn't a straw
that broke the camel's back.

Seen

For fifty-eight years
she's only seen
who I should have been.
My hair should be cut short
in a black pixie.
My job should be a nurse.
I should be in church on Saturdays.
I should be praying before meals.
I should be jewelry free.
I should be 2" shorter,
and hate cats.
She hated everything about me.
I live in sin,
a fornicator.
I am a drunk
with seven glasses of wine a week.
But last month
the doctors fixed her mangled heart.
Now she's asking about my work,
my relationships,
my hobbies,
even about my feelings.
She even remembers
what I tell her.
"I didn't know you took a writing class."
"You must know about a lot of things
to see all of those kinds of patients."
"You're so strong to race canoes."
"You look so happy."
"You and Mike really support each other."
Maybe she in there all along,
hiding her mother's love from me
until they fixed her loving place.

Heart Repair

Her palm humps the back
of her other hand.
The last time I was at a pre-admit,
I was having a child
of my own.
The flimsy dividers open the cubicles
to a common walkway.
Down the gauntlet
I hear
one HIPPA breach
after another.
A stray strip
of shredded patient info
is wedged under the signature pad,
connected to the monitor
up on the wall.
There's still a smudge of ink
I missed
when her frustrated hand
tried to sign
with a real pen.
"What?"
My mom looks at me.
"Crowns,"
I point to my teeth.
She turns back
to the woman across the desk.
"Oh yes. Gold. See?
They're going to take them out
for my daughter
before they cremate me."
I look down
and shuffle through the pile of paperwork
on my lap.
"Any urinary tract infections?"
"What?"
My mom turns toward me.
"UTIs?"
I shout.

"Oh," she replies.
"Not since I became a widow."
Bee Hive Hair laughs a short snort,
not sure if it's okay.
Of course, heart surgery
is no laughing matter.
Mom braces herself
to stand and sign her name
again.
Epoch stretches of census data
have passed
while we've been estranged.
Now we're here
at hospital admissions
sludging through
intakes and legal disclaimers.
Bee Hive leaves
to make a copy of Mom's insurance card.
My mom pats my hand
with her 85-year-old withered one.
"We're getting to know each other,"
she says,
"and I think,"
her eyes sparkle behind wrinkled lids,
"I think,
we like each other."

The End

www.ingramcontent.com/pod-product-compliance
Lightning Source LLC
Chambersburg PA
CBHW060800050426
42449CB00008B/1461